HEAVY METAL'S BIG FOUR

Scott Ian of Anthrax in the place where he's most comfortable—midair.

HEAVY METAL'S BIG FOUR

How Metallica, Megadeth, Anthrax, and Slayer Reshaped Metal

DANIEL BUKSZPAN

CONTENTS

INTRODUCTION

WARSAW, 2010

Every so often, the seemingly impossible happens. In June 2010, the four most popular thrash metal bands in the world—Anthrax, Megadeth, Metallica, and Slayer—united for a string of tour dates. Until then, no one believed it was possible.

Collectively, these bands are known as thrash metal's Big Four, and from 1981 through 1991, they were the genre's most popular emissaries. Decades later, they still are, and the series of concerts they played under the Big Four banner in 2010 and 2011 celebrated their longevity, survival, and improbable success.

Initially, the concept of any of these bands hitting the big time was absurd. The music was utterly uncommercial and ran counter to every prevailing musical trend the 1980s could cough up. I know this because I worked at a record store back then, and whenever I put on a Big Four band's album, customers would immediately ask my supervisor to take it off. They hated it.

The genre broke out of its dungeon when Metallica opened for Ozzy Osbourne's *The Ultimate Sin* tour in 1986. Ozzy fans became Metallica fans at those concerts and reported to the nearest record store to buy *Master of Puppets*, the album being promoted. While they were there, they would ask, "Are there any other bands like this?" There were, and the effect was immediate.

"We started in May '87, selling out clubs with five hundred to one thousand people," Anthrax guitarist Scott Ian told *Metal Hammer* in 2019. "Cut to December '87, we're headlining to upwards of seven thousand people a night."

Metallica went Top 10 with *. . . And Justice for All* in 1988, and the spotlight that shone on them also shone on the other three bands. Suddenly, their commercially unpalatable music was gaining attention. Mainstream press outlets were covering it. They were all on MTV. The records were selling, and the concerts were packed. There was even a test run for the 2010 Big Four dates when Anthrax, Megadeth, and Slayer played together on 1991's *Clash of the Titans* tour.

Then it was over. Metallica released their self-titled album, which went thermonuclear. It debuted at #1 and sold millions of copies, but instead of bringing Anthrax, Megadeth, and Slayer to the #1 spot with them, it actually signaled the end of the thrash metal movement. *Metallica* had abandoned that musical form entirely and new kinds of music were coming to the forefront, as they always do and always will. All things must pass.

Many lesser bands broke up amid these declining commercial fortunes, but these guys didn't. They put their heads down and kept going, the same way Metallica did when people called them sellouts who had forgotten where they came from. Every member of all four bands was a lifer who played this music because they loved it, and that attitude sustained them through the 1990s. Affection for metal began to reassert itself in the 2000s, so when Metallica began putting together the Big Four concerts in 2009, all the bands still had audiences. They had endured.

The Big Four have been in each other's orbits since 1981, and they have an intertwined history. They've been sharing stages in one configuration or another since the beginning. Slayer guitarist Kerry King was briefly in Megadeth. When Metallica's gear was stolen in 1984, Anthrax lent them their own. Additionally, there has been a massive beef between a couple of the bands over the years, and grudges that have lasted decades. In other words, they're just like family!

Perhaps aware that the "like family" dynamic can be a fraught one, Metallica wisely organized a dinner for the four bands on June 15, 2010, in Warsaw, the night before the first Big Four concert. If musician X was going to see musician Y and have ancient wounds reopened as a result, it was better that it happened at a private dinner than onstage.

Luckily, that didn't happen. There was a lot of happy reminiscing among the seventeen musicians, as well as simple gratitude for having survived the music industry's shenanigans. The Big Four concerts celebrated the fact that thirty years after coming up together, they were all still here, and on June 16, the night after the dinner, they could all bring the pain, just as they had in the 1980s.

The Big Four put the thrash metal genre into motion in 1981, and today, it's still an outsider movement, despite millions of copies sold of Anthrax's *Among the Living*, Megadeth's *Peace Sells . . . But Who's Buying?*, Metallica's *Master of Puppets*, and Slayer's *Reign in Blood*. Those records still sound like nothing else and are as radical today as they were during the Reagan era, so they keep selling and picking up new fans. As long as there are people out there for whom the Top 40 doesn't resonate, and who need something authentic that expresses their rage, these bands will never be irrelevant.

Ambassadors of the Big Four (*from left*: Kerry King of Slayer, Dave Mustaine of Megadeth, Scott Ian of Anthrax, and James Hetfield of Metallica) backstage at Warsaw's Sonisphere Festival on June 16, 2010. Getting these four bands on the same stage was a "pinch me" moment thirty years in the making.

(L–R) Slayer's Kerry King and Jeff Hanneman bring their Judas Priest-inspired twin guitar attack to snowy Montreal.

CHAPTER 1

1981: INFLUENCES AND FORMATION

The Big Four thrash metal bands are Anthrax, Megadeth, Metallica, and Slayer. Controversy may forever swirl as to which one is the best, but no one can dispute which is the first, chronologically and alphabetically.

BACILLUS ANTHRACIS

Anthrax was founded in the New York City borough of Queens on July 18, 1981, according to the band's official Facebook page. Guitarist Scott Ian and bassist Dan Lilker were the ones responsible.

Ian was born Scott Ian Rosenfeld, and unlike a lot of people who make their living playing thrash metal, he claimed no significant family traumas during his upbringing. In fact, he described his childhood in Queens as almost idyllic. "It was a great place to grow up," he told *Tablet* in 2011.

Queens was also home to the Ramones. As a heavy metal fan with a taste for punk, Ian had a special place in his heart for the foursome, who dressed more like teenage hoodlums than rock stars. They were relatable to him in ways his other musical heroes weren't.

"They were from Forest Hills, which was only six, seven miles away from where I lived," he recalled. "They seemed completely reachable, whereas Kiss—even though Gene Simmons's mom lived a mile from where I lived—seemed completely out of reach, in a different universe."

Ian said in his 2015 memoir, *I'm the Man: The Story of That Guy from Anthrax*, that he and Lilker knew each other from Bayside High School. The pair bonded over Judas Priest and Iron Maiden, heavy metal bands that were pushing the boundaries of volume and aggression established by Black Sabbath and AC/DC. These newer British guys had an even harder edge, and it was groundbreaking.

Anthrax owes its name to the fact that Lilker paid attention in science class. He had learned about the disease caused by *Bacillus anthracis*, and it became the band's namesake, because, as Ian put it, "it just sounded metal."

Despite their cool name, Anthrax was still not much more than a concept. In fact, Lilker told *Ultimate Metal* in 2008 that in that early incarnation, it was "just a high school band." No one else was as committed as they were, so members came and went.

Lilker's tenure in Anthrax proved impermanent as well. He left the band he cofounded in 1983 after recording their debut LP, *Fistful of Metal*. Still, Ian said Lilker was crucial to the band's founding, stating, "There is no Anthrax without Danny."

In the words of the Stimulators, "loud fast rules." The people who went on to play in the Big Four bands learned that truism from several pioneering bands that preceded them, such as the Ramones, Judas Priest, and Iron Maiden, among several others.

A MODEST BEGINNING

While Anthrax can cite its exact launch date, Metallica cannot. They formed in 1981, too, but no official date is associated with the event.

Drummer Lars Ulrich was born in Denmark and moved to Los Angeles at sixteen to train for a career in professional tennis. By his own account, he didn't even make it as far as his own high school team, but it didn't matter. He had discovered a band called Diamond Head, who were part of the New Wave of British Heavy Metal (NWOBHM) movement, and that took him down a rabbit hole from which he would never emerge.

Ulrich played drums, and like Lilker and Ian, he was also obsessed with the newest heavy metal coming out of England. It was faster and harder than anything he had ever heard before, and it really had teeth.

Like Anthrax, he had the band name Metallica before he had a band. It derived from his time on the tape-trading circuit, a vital resource for fans of up-and-coming metal bands in the pre-internet Stone Age. Back then, fans who wanted to learn about new, independent metal had to become pen pals with other fans and trade home-recorded cassettes through the mail.

These fans were diehards, and many founded their own fanzines to get the word out about the newest singles, EPs, and demos that were circulating. These makeshift publications were lifelines to anyone hungry for new metal. In 2023, Ulrich described the production values of the typical fanzine to the *SmartLess* podcast: "It was eight pages stapled together down at Kinko's about whatever their favorite French heavy metal band that five people had heard of," he said.

Ron Quintana, a heavy metal diehard from the San Francisco area, had connected with Ulrich via the tape-trading circuit. Ulrich told NPR that at "a kegger," Quintana told him he intended to start a fanzine. He was considering two different names: *Metallica* and *Metal Mania*. Ulrich suggested the latter, leaving the drummer free to use the former should he start his own band.

It meant his future band wouldn't have to use one of the other names that would be under consideration when the time came. According to *Metal Forces*, these included Nixon and Thunderfuck (and, honestly, the stranger choice is Nixon). Thus armed, Ulrich returned to Los Angeles and placed an ad in the *Recycler*, a local newspaper: "Drummer looking for other metal musicians to jam with. Tygers of Pan Tang, Diamond Head, and Iron Maiden."

A guitar player named James Hetfield responded. He had already been the vocalist for a band called Leather Charm, playing alongside bassist Ron McGovney. According to Mick Wall's 2010 book, *Enter Night—Metallica: The Biography*, his first meeting with Ulrich was unimpressive, to put it kindly. The guitarist was not complimentary toward his drumming and it seemed unlikely that anything would come of it.

But the drummer was nothing if not persistent. He kept after Hetfield and eventually convinced him to come to his house and spin records. This was the point at which the pair began to bond, and the timing would end up working in their favor.

One of Ulrich's fellow Southern California heavy metal zealots was Brian Slagel, who was producing a fanzine of his own but wanted to take his fandom one step further and start a record label. The intention was to sign underground bands from the area. Metal Blade Records' flagship release, the *Metal Massacre* compilation, would provide desperately needed exposure for some of these bands, none of whom had record labels chasing after them with contracts and fountain pens.

"Lars called me up and said, 'Hey, if I put together a band, can I be on your compilation album?'" Slagel recalled. "He called James and said, 'Hey, we can be on this record.'" It was a modest beginning.

HOW ABOUT "DRAGONSLAYER"?

Meanwhile, that Halloween in 1981, Slayer beat both Anthrax and Metallica to the punch by playing the first-ever gig by a Big Four band, a battle of the bands at the auditorium in South Gate, California. A hand-drawn flyer for the concert read, "Experience Slayer's assault on heavy metal." Admission was one dollar.

Slayer was also ahead of the pack when it came to their lineup. Metallica and Anthrax endured several personnel shifts before achieving stability (let's not even get started on Megadeth), but the first Slayer lineup was *really* the first Slayer lineup. Guitarists Jeff Hanneman and Kerry King, drummer Dave Lombardo, and bassist Tom Araya were all present and accounted for at the band's founding.

Like Anthrax and Metallica, Slayer's origin story dates back to 1981. King, then sixteen years old and still in high school, had played in a cover band alongside bassist and vocalist Araya. They did what high school cover bands do best and broke up, so he went to auditions in search of his next gig. In 1983, he told the fanzine *Whiplash* that was when he met Hanneman. "I was at an audition for another shitty LA band and Jeff happened to be auditioning for the same band," King said. "Our talents and interests were similar, so that's when Slayer started."

Lombardo was also sixteen and lived down the street from King. People who knew him to be a musician in search of a band gave him a hot tip—there was a house close by, and heavy metal guitar sounds emanated from it on a perpetual basis. Maybe he should swing by and tell whoever lived there that he was a drummer?

He swung by on his pizza delivery route and introduced himself to King, saying he wanted to start a band. After a few jams in the Lombardo family garage, King invited Hanneman to be part of it, then asked his former bandmate Araya to join. The original, classic Slayer lineup was complete, a configuration that would go on to make some of the band's greatest music.

As far as their name is concerned, the only choices were Wings of Fire and Slayer, and they wisely chose the latter. Despite the straightforward reality of the process, a pernicious urban legend has persisted, suggesting their name was a shortening of Dragonslayer. Sure, there's a 1981 swords-and-sorcery movie by that name depicting virgin sacrifices to a centuries-old dragon named Vermithrax Pejorative, and that certainly sounds like it could make for some compelling Slayer subject matter. But, as King told *FaceCulture* in 2006, there was not an iota of truth to the rumor. They were always Slayer.

Metallica is most often described as the Big Four band that kicked down the doors for the rest to follow. While that's plainly and objectively true, Slagel gave credit to Slayer, too, when he spoke with *Metal Hammer* in 2024. "Slayer were one of the bands that started that scene," Slagel said. "They helped drive a truck through everything, then a bunch of other bands came through after them."

Rumors alleging that Slayer originally named themselves after the 1981 fantasy film *Dragonslayer* are pernicious lies.

PROTOTYPES AND PREDECESSORS

WHENEVER A REPRESENTATIVE of one of the Big Four bands is asked who inspired them to start a band, certain artists are consistently cited in interview upon interview. Those breakneck tempos, chugging guitars, and double-bass 32nd notes may have been perfected by Anthrax, Megadeth, Metallica, and Slayer, but all freely acknowledge that they didn't invent any of it.

The following artists made music that got a bunch of young American musicians so hyped up they had to go out and try it themselves. There are others besides these ten (not enough can be said about the double-bass-drum intro to Accept's "Fast as a Shark"), but the artists listed here seem to come up most often whenever members of the Big Four bands are asked, "So, what made you want to play this type of music?"

Black Sabbath

"Bill, Geezer, Ozzy, and Tony, if it weren't for you, we wouldn't be here," Ulrich said when he and Hetfield inducted them into the Rock & Roll Hall of Fame in 2006. "If there was no Black Sabbath, there would be no Metallica."

Black Sabbath's influence on the Big Four is undisputable. It's almost an immutable law of nature: None of those bands would exist without that Birmingham quartet, and if you're a metal fan anywhere on the casual-to-obsessive spectrum, Black Sabbath laid the foundation beneath your feet.

Diamond Head

Metallica drummer Lars Ulrich is perhaps the most famous booster of Diamond Head, but he's not alone. Dave Mustaine of Megadeth told *SiriusXM* in 2023 that he was blown away by them, too.

"I thought they had a great singer, and I thought the guitar riffs were amazing," he said, adding that the Metallica lineup he was a part of covered several of their songs in the early days, such as "Helpless," "The Prince," and "Am I Evil?"

"People think those are original songs in Metallica, and they're not," he said. "They're Diamond Head songs."

Discharge

The British hardcore band Discharge played a crucial role in the development of thrash metal, if for no other reason than that they helped popularize the thrash beat. If, somehow, you don't know what that is, put on "Counterattack" by D.R.I. from the 1985 album *Dealing with It*—it's the reason the song is over and done with in a tidy eighteen seconds.

Scott Ian told *Vice* that Anthrax might not exist but for Discharge. His fellow bands in the Big Four probably wouldn't either. "I could list fifteen bands that if it wasn't for [*Hear Nothing, See Nothing, Say Nothing*], they possibly wouldn't even be bands," he said. "Without that Discharge album, I don't know what I would have done . . . we wouldn't have made the albums we made. We wouldn't have become the bands that created thrash metal."

OPPOSITE: Black Sabbath (*clockwise from top*: Ozzy Osbourne, Tony Iommi, Geezer Butler, and Bill Ward) influenced every Big Four band. Ozzy gave one of them, Metallica, their biggest break. ABOVE RIGHT: Diamond Head guitarist Brian Tatler in Malmö, Sweden, on October 16, 2022. BELOW RIGHT: A flyer for a performance by UK hardcore band Discharge, whose records made young thrash musicians follow Willie Nelson's advice and pick up the tempo.

K. K. Downing and Glenn Tipton of Judas Priest at London's Hammersmith Odeon in 1978. They pioneered the metallic dual-lead guitar sound that almost every thrash band with two guitarists eventually appropriated.

Judas Priest

Mustaine told *The Quietus* in 2016 that hearing Judas Priest's "Victim of Changes" more or less changed his life. "It was the heaviest thing I'd heard in my life up to that point . . . always loved K. K. Downing."

King said Priest was also a significant influence on Slayer. However, when it came to the British band's twin-guitar attack, he said that he was more of a Glenn Tipton guy than a K. K. Downing guy. He told *Rolling Stone* in 2022 that when he and Hanneman covered Priest songs together, they had a scientific method to determine who played which lead: "[Hanneman] would always play the K. K. Downing guitar parts because he was the blond guy."

Iron Maiden's second album, *Killers*, features several songs that could be described as pre-thrash. "Purgatory," in particular, is just a few bpm away.

Kim Bendix Petersen, a.k.a. King Diamond, lead singer for Mercyful Fate. Gene Simmons of Kiss sent him a cease-and-desist letter for the makeup because, of course, he did.

Iron Maiden

Iron Maiden's sound came really close to thrash metal a few times on their first couple of records. See "Purgatory" from 1981's *Killers* for an example.

Ulrich told Zane Lowe of *Apple Music* in 2020 that of all the classic metal bands, Maiden influenced them the most. King also sang Maiden's praises, telling *Rolling Stone* in 2017 that he loved 1982's *The Number of the Beast*, saying singer Bruce Dickinson's performance "stomped all over everybody's guts."

Interestingly, on the list of favorite singers Hetfield provided to *Rolling Stone*, he chose the guy Dickinson replaced, Paul Di'Anno—and nobody picks Paul Di'Anno. It just goes to show how vital those first two Maiden records were in informing Metallica's sound, right down to the vocals.

Mercyful Fate

Denmark's Mercyful Fate trafficked in occult subject matter that Anthrax, Megadeth, and Metallica pretty pointedly avoided. Slayer, on the other hand, poured it on and kept it coming.

"There was definitely a Mercyful Fate influence on *Hell Awaits*," King told *Rolling Stone* in 2017. "You can tell by the super long songs with, like, ten thousand riff changes."

The band was led by singer King Diamond, who wore face paint so reminiscent of that worn by Kiss bassist Gene Simmons that he was threatened with a lawsuit for it, according to *Metal Hammer*. Additionally, his singing voice is the most acquired of tastes. His fans love it, but if you're not on board, it sounds like an obnoxious parody of Rob Halford by someone who hates Rob Halford.

Lemmy Kilmister of Motörhead on November 27, 1981, in Stockholm during the *Ace of Spades* tour. Without this band, a young Lars Ulrich would never have heard the song "Overkill" and been tempted to try that double bass himself.

A flyer for a concert by the Ramones from Queens, *Noo Yawk*. Note that openers Van Halen are in tow and that the evening set ticket buyers back a whole $5.

Motörhead

While Lars Ulrich said there would be no Metallica without Black Sabbath, Hetfield told *Newsweek* in 2017 that there's "no Metallica without a Motörhead."

Ulrich said that he became a believer the moment he first heard them. "I was in a record store and the double-bass intro to 'Overkill' started, and I never heard anything like that in my life," he said. He added that being a Motörhead fan also gave him a feeling of being a part of something bigger, and he wanted his own band to create a similar feeling of community among fans.

"That was what Motörhead represented," he said. "You were a part of a gang . . . we all had a common connection where we felt like we all belonged. . . . There was no separation between band and fans. . . . That unity made me just want to be in a band and be part of that collective and do my own version of that experience."

Ramones

In the 1970s, you didn't get much louder, faster, or snottier than the Ramones. During their CBGB heyday, they were the foremost purveyors of blink-and-you-missed-it anthems that were equal parts bubblegum pop and ruthless brutality. "It makes everybody else look so bullshit and wimpy," Lou Reed said upon first hearing "Blitzkrieg Bop" in 1975. "They really hit where it hurts."

Parents in the 1980s likely hated the sound of thrash metal as much as their 1970s counterparts hated the Ramones, and for similar reasons. Both led with an approach that rejected classic rock, and both created a buzzsaw-guitar noise that rejected FM radio Clapton-isms and turned the instrument into something explosive. In both cases, audience members either embraced the new sound or fled the venue.

Raven

In 2024, Scott Ian told *Classic Rock* that Raven's "Hellraiser/Action" was an example of thrash "before thrash existed." Calling them "a really fast New Wave of British Heavy Metal group," Anthrax had the privilege of sharing stages with them on many occasions, and the guitarist had fond reminiscences of their drummer, Rob "Wacko" Hunter.

"The guy wore a hockey goalie helmet onstage and definitely earned his name, smashing his head into his cymbals, mic stands, walls, and anyone he was having any sort of dispute with," he said.

Venom

Venom was loud, fast, raw, and not particularly technical. King described them to *Rolling Stone* in 2017 as "the best shitty band ever," and it's plain to see the influence they had on Slayer's lyrics—Venom sang, "We drink the vomit of the priests," and Slayer had their own "What's grosser than gross?" songs to match them.

Ulrich also name-checked Venom, telling *Metal Hammer* in 2019 that their influence resulted in one of their most enduring songs, "Whiplash."

"One of the bands we were listening to, who were an influence on 'Whiplash,' was Venom," he said. "Songs like 'Angel Dust' and 'Live Like an Angel (Die Like a Devil)' . . . Venom need to get name-checked more when people talk about Metallica's early days."

TOP: Raven (*from left*: Mark Gallagher, Rob "Wacko" Hunter, and John Gallagher) from the United Kingdom, whose up-tempo metal helped create the blueprint for thrash. BOTTOM: All hail the mighty Venom (*from left*: Dave "Abaddon" Bray, Conrad "Cronos" Lant, and Jeffrey "Mantas" Dunn)! What they lacked in technical proficiency, they made up for with tour-bus pee-pee incidents.

Dave Mustaine with Metallica at the Paramount Theater in Staten Island, New York.

CHAPTER 2

1982: "METTALLICA"

Metallica's Cliff Burton, James Hetfield, and numerous Marshall stacks wage all-out war on the eardrums of those in attendance at Willy's in Sayreville, New Jersey.

In 1982, Slayer was in the same boat as most fledgling bands. They had a rough idea of what they wanted to accomplish stylistically, but they just weren't there yet, so now it was a matter of going onstage and working out the bugs.

It was also a matter of separating themselves from the Los Angeles Sunset Strip scene. Its prevailing artistic sensibility was exemplified by Dokken, Mötley Crüe, and Ratt, among others, so King told *Metal Hammer* in 2016 that Slayer usually played an hour south of Los Angeles, where they were more welcome. "We played more in Orange County, where there was more of a metal stronghold," he said. "We sort of exiled ourselves to Anaheim."

Hanneman told *Guitar World* that in 1982, as Slayer was finding its way musically, his newfound fascination with punk almost threatened to muscle out his interest in metal. Instead, it became an integral part of the band's music. "That's how Slayer's sound came together—it's the speed of punk combined with the big riffs of metal," he said.

Meanwhile, Metallica had prioritized recording "Hit the Lights" to four-track with the most threadbare version of the band imaginable: Ulrich on drums and Hetfield on guitar, bass, and vocals.

Lead guitar was recorded at the last minute by one Lloyd Grant at his apartment. He told *Rockzone Legends* in 2016 that he had responded to Ulrich's *Recycler* ad even before Hetfield did. He had casually jammed with Ulrich a handful of times and had rehearsed "Hit the Lights" twice or maybe three times with Hetfield on bass. "[Ulrich] called me and said they were gonna be on this compilation album and he brought over a tape of 'Hit the Lights' recorded on a four-track and asked me to make some solos for that," Grant said. Hetfield told *Blabbermouth* in 2016 that Grant nailed it in one take.

Delivering the finished recording to Slagel was as last-minute as it gets. In the 1993 book *Metallica Unbound*, author and prominent tape trader K. J. Doughton said that as Hetfield and Ulrich were on their way to deliver the recording to Slagel, they made a short pit stop at Grant's house to pick up a guitar solo, as one might make a detour to pick up milk at 7-11. "The band screeched into Grant's driveway, lugged the four-track into his front room, and watched him churn a second lead break," Doughton wrote. "The 'Hit the Lights' recipe was now complete."

Early on in the same year, Metallica assembled a lineup that could perform live. Ron McGovney, who had played with Hetfield in Leather Charm, joined on bass, and Dave Mustaine joined as lead guitarist. Mustaine told *The Shawn Ryan Show* that he had seen an ad in the *Recycler* seeking a lead guitar player, and when he responded to the phone number in the ad, Ulrich picked up. They discussed their influences, and the guitarist mentioned the Welsh band Budgie. The drummer was awestruck. Budgie was as popular in the United States in 1982 as Saxon was—which is to say, not at all. Just knowing the band's name was a big deal.

He went to an audition at McGovney's house, where Hetfield was also living. He set up his guitar and amp and started warming up, but after a while, he noticed the other three still hadn't come into the rehearsal room. "I said, 'Guys, are we gonna do the audition?'" he recalled. "They said, 'You got the gig.'" Just turning on an amp and getting his fingers limber for a couple of minutes had done it.

The lineup in place, Metallica's first gig was on March 14, 1982, at an Anaheim venue called Radio City. In 2019, Ulrich posted the flyer for the gig to Instagram, along with a handwritten set list and diary entry. "1st ever gig," the diary said. "Very nervous. Only band. Dave broke a string on the first song. Played 50-50!!! Went down pretty good."

Admission was $15, and the nine-song set featured seven NWOBHM covers, four of which were by Diamond Head, as well as two originals, "Hit the Lights" and "Jump in the Fire." The flyer promised that you could see the band again just twelve days later

Slayer (L-R: Jeff Hanneman, Dave Lombardo, Tom Araya, and Kerry King) perform to an appreciative sea of fists, devil horns, and leather.

SUICIDAL

ABOVE: Kirk Hammett, James Hetfield, and Cliff Burton at Sports 9 Arena in Old Bridge, New Jersey. The venue also offered ice skating to its patrons.
OPPOSITE: Anthrax (*clockwise from left*: Charlie Benante, Frank Bello, Joey Belladonna, Dan Spitz, and Scott Ian) flaunt their gnarly decks and chiseled biceps.

at a venue called Woodstock. It also teased the forthcoming *Metal Massacre* compilation. As it turned out, they would share the bill that night with another newly formed band, Slayer.

"The place we played with them was kind of a local hole-in-the-wall," Ulrich told *Metal Hammer* in 2024. "They weren't 'Angel of Death' Slayer yet, but they were on their way, certainly . . . you could definitely feel that this was a musical force to be reckoned with."

This would be a magnificent opportunity to say that at this gig, the two bands struck up a close friendship that acted as the everlasting concrete foundation for the Big Four. Unfortunately, that would be a lie. There was no problem between the bands, but there was no close connection either. There was, however, a spirit of healthy competition.

"Metallica and Slayer didn't really have that much of a relationship, but they were both interested in what the other was doing," Slagel told *Metal Hammer* in 2024. "Whenever I'd hang out with Metallica, they'd go, 'What does this new Slayer stuff sound like? How fast is it?' And vice versa with Slayer. They were in a covert race to see who could write the heavier, faster album."

When *Metal Massacre* was released on June 14, 1982, it was a humiliating disappointment. Not because the sound quality is crap, which it absolutely is. And not because Ulrich sounds like a ten-year-old with two lessons under his belt. Nor was it because Hetfield's vocals could politely be described as "pitchy." No, it was because the band got listed on the back cover as "Mettallica," with two *Ts*.

No1

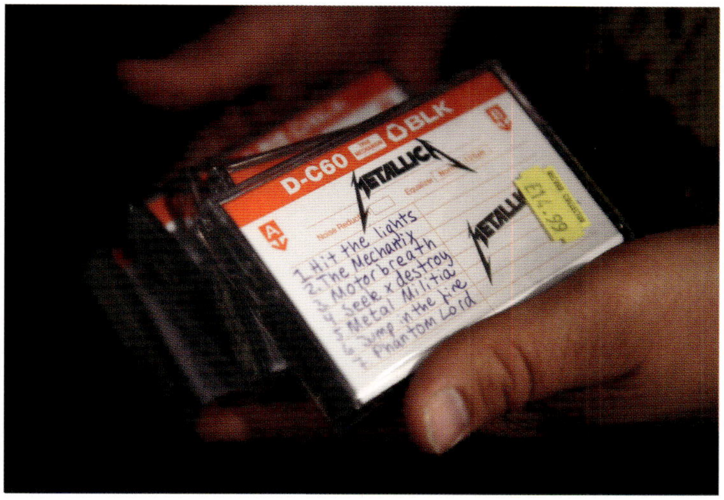

ABOVE: It's April 17, 2015, and an employee of the Record Collector music shop in Sheffield cradles copies of Metallica's reissued 1982 demo tape, *No Life 'til Leather*, close to his loving bosom. TOP: James Hetfield holds down a D chord at L'Amour East in Elmhurst, Queens. OPPOSITE: Scott Ian of Anthrax at L'Amour, "The Rock Capital of Brooklyn."

Undeterred, the band set about recording another demo in July. Dubbed *No Life 'til Leather*, it furiously made the rounds on the tape-trading circuit. And what's more, their name was spelled correctly on the cassette cover.

Similar growing pains were afoot 3,000 miles away in Bayside, Queens. Scott Ian and Dan Lilker were trying to create a stable lineup for Anthrax, and they had secured lead guitarist Greg Walls and drummer Greg D'Angelo. Ian's former schoolmate, Neil Turbin, became the vocalist after a few people had come and gone, including Ian's younger brother, Jason.

With a lineup in place, the band hit the New York City club circuit. They recorded a demo that year and even performed on a Manhattan public-access cable TV show called *Unique NY Talent Showcase 1982*. (Their performance of "Satan's Wheels" is available on YouTube and is worth seeking out for its open-mic production values.)

THE MAGICAL, MYSTICAL PRACTICE OF TAPE TRADING

TOM G. WARRIOR of the Swiss thrash band Celtic Frost was once a young metal fan named Thomas Gabriel Fischer. The local record store didn't stock the independent records he'd heard about, but that was okay. He was part of the tape-trading circuit, a network of deeply committed fans willing to go much further than the average listener to keep up with underground metal.

The tape-trading circuit was essential to getting the word out to hardcore fans, many of whom would go on to form bands of their own, such as Ulrich and Ian. Their own bands had to be tenacious in order to be heard, and Fischer said you had to be equally determined to be part of the network of people who were circulating this music among each other. "You had to prove that you're a fanatic," he told *Metal Injection* in 2023. "You had to drive to record stores in other cities to see if they had one single record that they imported, or you had to find the right addresses for tape traders; you had to really put an effort into discovering music and you had to show that you really mean it."

That kind of next-level fandom is impossible to imagine today mainly because technology has rendered it obsolete. Your favorite streaming service is happy to turn you on to as many Estonian blackened doom bands as you want in one sitting, all at the click of a link. You don't even have to venture outdoors. But back in tape trading's heyday, fans had to take out ads in fanzines to find trading partners with whom to swap demos, singles, or otherwise obscure new metal, all on homemade cassettes.

One could not benefit from tape trading passively. You had to pay it forward, so when your friend from Cleveland sent a cassette copy of an unsigned metal band's demo to your home in Dallas (on their dime), you were expected to make a cassette copy of your own, package it, and mail it off to your friend in Bayonne (on your dime). That person would, in turn, keep it going.

It was what people like Fischer had to do to stay in the loop, and what's most amazing about it is that it worked. There was a maniacal hunger among fans for this music that made the practice function. Buying stamps, mailers, and blank cassettes, then waiting in line at the post office was a small price to pay to be looped in. It was worth it when you opened your mailbox and saw a manila envelope with your name on it and a cassette inside.

Every Big Four band acknowledges that the tape-trading circuit was pivotal to their careers. *No Life 'til Leather* famously benefited from the circuit, as King told *Guitar World* in 2024. "Metallica's demo got passed around, big time," he said. "We all had that."

Ulrich was also part of the circuit. In 1984, he told journalist and celebrated tape trader Bernard Doe of *Metal Forces* that sending *No Life 'til Leather* to the right people ensured the demo would get heard. "I knew that by sending them to all the principal tape traders—like K. J. Doughton, Patrick Scott, and yourself—that they would send them to ten or twenty more people and it would just kind of spread out into an underground following," he said.

As tempting as it is to compare tape trading to file sharing, the comparison is highly flawed. People in the network actually bought the records after hearing the cassette copies they had been mailed. Tape trading put money in the pockets of the artists, if circuitously.

Though technology has rendered tape trading obsolete, Fischer said that while he saw upsides to streaming platforms, the charm of the tape-trading subculture and the attendant joy of discovery had been lost in the upgrade. "There's good things and bad things about [streaming], but yeah, the magic, of course, the mystique is lacking," he told *Metal Injection* in 2023. "I lament that of course . . . it was magical."

Dear Gen Z, these contraptions are called "blank cassettes," and they were instrumental in the underground metal tape-trading circuit. It would have been very hard to get the word out about the Big Four without these doodads.

Cliff Burton uses his hair and his Rickenbacker to obscure James Hetfield at the Fountain Casino in Aberdeen, New Jersey.

Unfortunately, McGovney was already finding himself on the outs with Metallica. In 2018, he told *Vintage Heavy Metal* that while he, Hetfield, and Ulrich all drank alcohol quite enthusiastically, Mustaine seemed to have more of a struggle with it. "He would sometimes just get so loaded that he was out of control," McGovney said. "It wasn't good whenever he got like that."

McGovney found himself on the receiving end of Mustaine's drunken ire on more than one occasion, and he felt like Hetfield and Ulrich didn't back him up when that happened. He recalled that, once, the guitarist poured beer into his bass. Another time, he tried to intervene during an altercation that saw Mustaine punch Hetfield in the face. "I jumped on Dave's back and he threw me over into a coffee table," he said. "We kicked him out of the band right there."

When he was reinstated with no consequences the next day, the bassist said in a 1997 interview that it was emblematic of the lopsided dynamic in the band. Despite already having a friendship with Hetfield, he felt much less important to the cofounders than Mustaine was. He said Hetfield and Ulrich would habitually take the lead guitarist's side despite the fact that Mustaine could be, as McGovney put it, "an asshole." "What really hurt me was James, because he was my friend and he was siding with them, and I suddenly became the outcast in the band," McGovney said, according to *Ultimate Metallica*.

McGovney and Metallica parted ways in December 1982, leaving them without a bass player. Luckily, they had seen a San Francisco band called Trauma at the Whisky a Go Go and were

Despite the advice of most guitar instructors, Kerry King of Slayer has eschewed trimming the strings protruding from his headstock.

transfixed by the bassist, Cliff Burton. Burton played like no bassist before or since. His sound was massively overdriven, he used a wah pedal, and he even engaged in the act of shredding, which is really hard to do on a bass's thick strings. Basically, he did everything people thought only guitar players could do. They had to have him in Metallica. They had to.

As it turned out, they had good timing. In a February 1986 interview, the bassist stated that when Metallica approached him, he was already considering leaving Trauma to pursue something uncompromising. "It was starting to get a little commercial in different ways, just different general musical attitudes that I found annoying," he said.

He had one condition. He would join only if the band moved to the Bay Area. As it turned out, to the guys in Metallica, that wasn't an ultimatum. It was a signing bonus. There was a burgeoning thrash scene in San Francisco and Metallica already knew from playing there several times that it was a much better fit for them than Los Angeles.

"We were drawing something like six hundred or so at every gig and making money out of it, which was something we had never done in LA," Ulrich told *Metal Forces* in 1984. When they relocated, they found themselves embraced by a local thrash metal scene that was happy to accept them as they were. The contrast with LA couldn't have been more clear. "It was great up there," the drummer said.

THE LABELS THAT MADE IT HAPPEN

MAJOR RECORD LABELS in 1982 had no idea thrash metal existed, and if they did, they didn't acknowledge it. This left independent labels to give these bands their first airing, and those labels generally had a lot in common with the bands in that they had boundless passion but no money.

The label owners put themselves in difficult financial straits to get these bands more visibility, and they did it for the same reason the bands played: It was a labor of love. Why else would they pile into a van and drive for hours to play in front of ten people at one in the morning on a Tuesday? It certainly wasn't for the money. And while the labels required capital to keep the lights on, they weren't in it for the money either. There was a higher calling.

"We were just young kids getting this music out there," Slagel told *Metal Hammer* in 2024. "None of us in that scene ever expected any of this stuff to happen to any of these bands."

Metal Blade founder Brian Slagel took his inspiration form British DJ Neal Kay's 1980 compilation, *Metal for Muthas* and the leg up that it gave Iron Maiden.

The flagship volume of the *Metal Massacre* compilation, which introduced ten new underground metal bands to the world, including Bitch, Cirith Ungol, and a group immortalized in the liner notes as "Mettallica."

Metal Blade Records

Metal Blade Records founder Brian Slagel was a NWOBHM fan who worked at Los Angeles's Oz Records and published his own fanzine, the *New Heavy Metal Revue*. New bands were emerging in Southern California with a distinctly British flavor, and he wanted to do for them what British DJ Neal Kay had done for Iron Maiden in 1980 by including that band on the *Metal for Muthas* compilation.

"It just seemed like I could help them out and have some fun at the same time, and that compilation was the first *Metal Massacre*," he said on the label's official website.

The compilation sold out quickly. Slagel had existing connections with distributors from working at Oz Records, and furthermore, fans of this music now had something they could walk into a store and buy.

Slagel told *Metal Sucks* that he borrowed money from his aunt to start the label and operated it out of his mother's San Fernando Valley garage. Slowly and methodically, it paid off, and the bands who won their first public exposure through the *Metal Massacre* compilations said they owed Slagel a lot. "Without Brian's openness to some raunchy teens with a crap-sounding cassette tape, we would be who knows where, and playing who knows what," Hetfield said.

Slayer contributed the track "Aggressive Perfector" to the label's 1983 compilation, *Metal Massacre III*. Like Hetfield, King said it was crucial to Slayer's career. "Without Metal Blade, there is a damn good chance we never would've made it out of LA," he said.

Eventually, Metal Blade grew to the point where Slagel could sign artists from the worldwide underground metal scene, such as King Diamond. The former Mercyful Fate vocalist said the label was instrumental in cultivating his long career. "There's a genuine love for metal there," the singer said. "Through staying true to that and doing their own thing, they've carved out a very specific niche that they control, and as an artist, it's wonderful to be a part of that."

Slayer contributed the track "Aggressive Perfector" to Metal Blade's 1983 compilation, *Metal Massacre III* and like Metallica, cited the compilation and label as crucial to Slayer's career.

Combat Records signed notable thrash bands like Nuclear Assault, Dark Angel, and Exodus (pictured). A distro deal with Germany's Noise Records brought international thrash bands like Voivod and Celtic Frost to US shores.

Megaforce Records

Megaforce Records was founded by husband and wife Jon and Marsha Zazula. They owned Rock n' Roll Heaven, a stall that sold records out of a flea market in East Brunswick, New Jersey. Despite not having their own dedicated brick-and-mortar store, they had a loyal customer base for underground metal, including a couple of kids from Queens in a band called Anthrax.

Jon Zazula was hooked into the tape-trading circuit, so a cassette by an unsigned band called Metallica found its way into his hands. It was the *No Life 'til Leather* demo, and when he played it for the first time, he decided he had to be a part of it, somehow.

He tried to get them signed to an existing label, but nobody would touch them. They were too loud, too fast, and there was no smoothing their rough edges. You might as well try to rehabilitate GG Allin. Forget it.

With no takers, the Zazulas founded Megaforce Records and put out Metallica's debut LP themselves. They had to refinance their house and max out all their credit cards to do it, but their belief in the band justified the financial burden. Jon Zazula said it took the full resources of both him and Marsha to make everything happen. He wasn't just talking about money, either—her day-to-day efforts were integral to the label's success and to the bands it signed. "Anything I couldn't figure out, she figured out," he told *Kerrang!* in 2019. "Between us we were able to make it happen."

Marsha Zazula passed away in 2021. *The New York Times* quoted her final interview with the website *Metal Voice*, in which she sounded proud of what she and her husband had accomplished against long odds. "We took ourselves out of a comfortable place, rolled the dice—had nothing to lose but nothing to gain necessarily—and put our hearts and souls into doing it," she said.

A little over a year later, Jon Zazula passed away. Metallica released a statement on Twitter to commemorate him, Marsha, and all the couple had accomplished. "In 1982, when no one wanted to take a chance on four kids from California playing a crazy brand of metal, Jonny and Marsha did, and the rest, as they say, is history," the statement read.

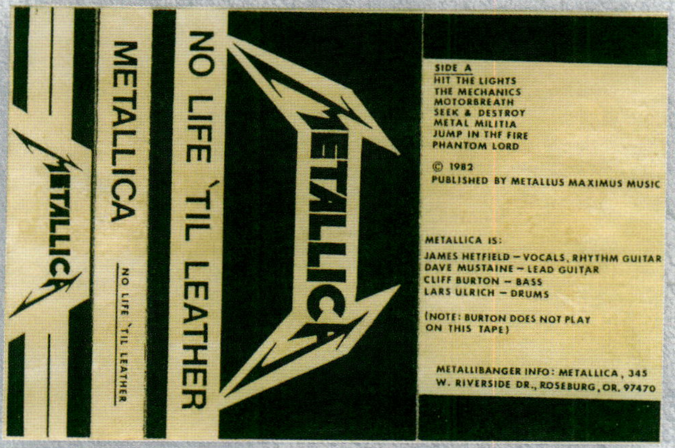

The Xerox-copied and scissor-cut insert that came with the *No Life 'til Leather* demo tape. Apologies to readers whose OCD is triggered by things that are off-center.

Combat Records

When Megadeth was formed in 1983, they were two years behind Metallica, Slayer, and Anthrax. Their debut album, *Killing Is My Business . . . and Business Is Good!*, emerged in 1985 on Combat Records.

Combat was not a passion project. It was a subsidiary of Important Record Distributors, which was created in response to Metallica's success on Megaforce. So, unlike Metal Blade and Megaforce, it was founded because there was an opening in the market that those other two labels had been instrumental in creating.

Megadeth became Combat Records recording artists on the strength of their 1984 demo, *Last Rites*. The Zazulas had expressed interest, but there was just too much baggage between Mustaine and his former band, who was signed to their label. Ultimately, Megadeth settled on Combat for a simple reason: Combat offered them the most money.

While the members of Anthrax, Metallica, and Slayer all showered their fledgling labels with praise and gratitude for taking a chance on them, similarly nostalgic statements about Combat from Megadeth are seemingly nonexistent. In fairness, there is also scant mention of the joys of working with Megadeth on the part of anyone affiliated with Combat.

Nevertheless, the label went on to do great things for thrash metal. They signed Nuclear Assault, Dark Angel, and Exodus, and entered into a deal with Germany's Noise Records to distribute its releases in the United States. This brought groundbreaking albums by international thrash bands like Voivod and Celtic Frost to American shops.

Mustaine and company may not sing Combat's praises, but the label's contribution to thrash metal as a genre is carved in stone.

James Hetfield and Dave Mustaine of Metallica share some onstage harmony on April 8, 1983, in Staten Island. T-minus three days until Mustaine was sent packing.

CHAPTER
3

1983: PURE, UNADULTERATED, WONDERFUL NOISE

Metallica (*from left*: James Hetfield, Lars Ulrich, Kirk Hammett, and Cliff Burton) give collective stink eye to some unidentified off-camera terror in Zwolle, Netherlands.

By February 1983, the members of Metallica were settling into life in Northern California. Hetfield and Ulrich stayed at the home of Mark Whitaker, who managed the local thrash metal band Exodus. Mustaine stayed at Whitaker's grandmother's house, an hour away from the El Cerrito home known as "the Metallica Mansion."

He didn't know the clock was ticking. In two months, he would be kicked out by the bandmates he called "brothers-in-arms" in his memoir. The way he saw it, they were soldiers on a dangerous but vital mission, and he was happy to dedicate his life to them. "I would have done anything for them," he said.

Their first gig with Burton was on March 5, 1983, at a San Francisco club called the Stone. In contrast to Los Angeles, the band felt at home there. They didn't have to make a place alongside the Sunset Strip bands, whom they loathed. Instead, there were bands like Exodus and another called Legacy, who would later change their name to Testament. They fit right in.

In April, they piled into a Winnebago with a U-Haul trailer and drove east. Upon hearing the *No Life 'til Leather* demo, record merchants Jon and Marsha Zazula founded Megaforce Records and signed the band, cobbling together every cent they could scrape up to pay for studio time. This meant no hotels, so the band moved into the Music Building in Jamaica, Queens.

It was not a place to live. It was a rehearsal space, one Scott Ian described in his memoir as "a fucking shithole." When he and Dan Lilker met Metallica for the first time, they instantly identified with them. "We were both in the same boat," he said. "We were no-name bands trying to do something real."

ABOVE: *Bon soir!* Dan Spitz and Scott Ian of Anthrax in Canada, supporting Raven in 1984. Might they be playing "Metal Thrashing Mad"? RIGHT: Slayer frontman Tom Araya used his earnings as a respiratory therapist to help finance the recording of their debut album, *Show No Mercy*.

While Metal Blade's Brian Slagel said the members weren't really BFFs, Slayer (*from left*: Kerry King, Dave Lombardo, Jeff Hanneman, and Tom Araya) semi-convincingly feign camaraderie for the cameras anyway.

Even though Metallica had just gotten there, Mustaine was about to play his last show with them on April 9. The gig was at L'Amour in Brooklyn, located just steps from the disco depicted in the movie *Saturday Night Fever*. They were playing with the Rods and Vandenberg, and Ian said an "already hammered" Mustaine was loudly and obnoxiously antagonizing Vandenberg during their afternoon sound check. "As soon as they ended a song, he started screaming at them that they sucked and they should get the fuck off the stage," Ian said. "Jonny Z pulled him away."

Two days later, on the morning of April 11, Mustaine awoke to the sight of his brothers-in-arms glaring down at him. He could tell it was bad news but he didn't understand how bad until Ulrich gave it to him. He was out of the band, effective immediately. Since his now-former bandmates and their label couldn't afford to fly him back home, the best they could do was put him on a Greyhound bus, which was leaving in one hour.

Hetfield, whom he characterized as his closest friend in the band, drove him to Manhattan's Port Authority bus terminal in complete silence. He said there were tears in Hetfield's eyes when they parted ways.

Due to the band's dire financial straits, he was not given any money to keep him fed during the bus ride. He was penniless, alone, and facing a four-day bus trip with nothing to do but seethe and starve. He had only his guitar and a bag of dirty clothes to share the misery with him.

Metallica frontman James Hetfield conveys some sort of dire musical tidings to the enthralled on August 5, 1983, at L'Amour East.

Chainmail enthusiast and original Anthrax singer Neil Turbin at Montreal's Spectrum.

One good thing came out of it. At some point, he looked down at the floor of the bus and saw a pamphlet about nuclear proliferation. One line jumped out at him, which used a word signifying the death of one million people from a nuclear explosion. "The arsenal of megadeath can't be rid no matter what the peace treaties come to," it read.

After Mustaine had been put on the bus, Ian went to the Music Building to rehearse, oblivious to what had happened. Burton gave him the news. The sound check incident at L'Amour had been simply one indignity of many that the band endured, and ousting the guitarist had been planned long in advance.

Ian was surprised by the decision, since he considered Mustaine to be the driving artistic force of the band. At the same time, he said the guitarist could be "an out-of-control, mean drunk," and while everyone in Metallica drank regularly, they could keep it together most of the time. On the other hand, when their now-former lead guitarist drank too much, he was impossible to deal with in a civilized way. Still, it didn't diminish anything he had accomplished in Metallica. "The guy is arguably the godfather of thrash metal," he said. "He wrote a lot of the riffs on *Kill 'Em All* and even some of *Ride the Lightning*. Without Dave Mustaine, maybe thrash metal never would have happened."

Ulrich explained to *Metal Forces* in 1984 why the decision had been made. Metallica may have been branded "Alcoholica" by fans for their hard-partying ways, but Mustaine's behavior while under the influence simply caused too many problems, no matter how well he played guitar. "When he had had a few to drink, he would become extremely obnoxious and very hard to control," the drummer said. "He put us in some very embarrassing situations."

Decades later, Mustaine told *Metal Hammer* that as hurtful and traumatic as it had been to be kicked out of the band, he understood the position the other three were in and took responsibility for his behavior. He acknowledged becoming violent when he drank, and he said at that time he was "kinda drunk 24/7." "I would have done the same thing as Metallica did," he said. "I had a problem with alcohol, and it cost me my job and cost me two very dear friends."

With the grim task of excusing Mustaine from further duty now in the rearview mirror, Metallica had another predicament. They had studio time booked to record the debut album they had driven 3,000 miles to make. Furthermore, there were gigs lined up, starting that Friday, and it was Monday.

Exodus lead guitarist Kirk Hammett was asked to come in from San Francisco to join the band so they could keep their commitments. As it turned out, he was already the proud owner of the *No Life 'til Leather* demo, so he already knew all the songs.

In 2014, Hammett told *Metal Hammer* that he got the call to audition for Metallica on April Fool's Day, leading him to believe it was a joke. Furthermore, he got the call while he was sitting on the toilet.

Upon realizing it was not a holiday prank, he said yes and flew out to meet the band on April 11, the same day the band had handed Mustaine his bus ticket. He told *Far Out* in 2024 that he got to the Music Building at seven o'clock that night and the whole band was only just waking up.

"I thought, 'Wow, I like these guys,'" he said.

It was mutual. The band set up and when Hammett played the solo to "Seek and Destroy" at the audition, they breathed a collective sigh of relief. He was the guy. That was a good thing, because there was no time for other arrangements if his playing had sucked.

A month later, Anthrax was dealing with lineup issues of its own. Their drummer, Greg D'Angelo, had left the group. A friend of Ian's told him about a drummer named Charlie Benante, who had extraordinary double-bass skills, to the extent that he could play the opening to Accept's "Fast as a Shark." In fact, he could play it faster than the record. Ian and Lilker sought him out, making the epic trek from Queens to the Bronx. The audition was everything the cofounders had hoped for. "We played 'Invaders' and 'Phantom of the Opera' from Iron Maiden and some songs from Judas Priest and Motörhead, and he nailed them all," Ian said.

Benante was also a songwriter. He contributed a new song called "Soldiers of Metal" almost immediately after joining, and lead guitarist Dan Spitz followed shortly thereafter. He was a guitar store clerk whom Ian had met while ogling gear, and he could play very well.

With $1,500 Ian had saved up, Anthrax went to Sonic Studios to record "Soldiers of Metal" and re-record some songs from their 1982 demo. They emerged with five tracks, and when he presented the recordings to Jon Zazula, he loved it and signed them to Megaforce.

The timing played out so that Anthrax was able to open the five Metallica shows that served as Hammett's inauguration. He made his debut at the Showplace in Dover, New Jersey, on April 16, 1983, just five days after Mustaine's ouster, with Anthrax in a support slot.

Slayer was likewise slugging it out in Los Angeles, playing club gigs and even house parties. Slayer had also recorded a demo, which entered the tape-trading network in short order. One copy made it to Bernard Doe, who gave it a frenzied review in *Metal Forces*. What the review lacked in punctuation it made up for in euphoric mania. "Slayer combine the speed and enthusiasm of Metallica with the Satanism of Venom to produce a barrage of black metallic death, most evident on the track 'Fight Till Death'; a truly frenzied attack of mayhem from beginning to end," he wrote.

The three songs on the demo were slated to appear on the band's forthcoming Metal Blade debut. Slagel saw them open for Bitch at the Woodstock club, where they were now seasoned veterans. He was particularly impressed by their rendition of Iron Maiden's "Phantom of the Opera." "I just went backstage and told them I have this little record label and if they wanted to do a track I'd put them on *Metal Massacre*," he said. The song "Aggressive Perfector" appeared on *Metal Massacre III*, and he signed them to Metal Blade to make a full-length LP.

Anthrax, Metallica, and Slayer were all making moves and seeing their careers improve, but Mustaine was having difficulty adjusting to life after Metallica. Getting fired and dumped on a bus one hour later was a gut punch. He had made enormous sacrifices to be in that band and lost everything.

Returning to his friends at home didn't provide the healing embrace he had hoped for. All of them knew what had happened, so reconnecting with them was not an exercise in comfort. Every time the topic came up, it ripped open the wound all over again.

Then it got significantly worse. On July 25, 1983, Metallica's debut album, *Kill 'Em All*, was released. When he was fired, Mustaine had asked them not to use the music he had written, but four of the album's ten songs were either by him or cowritten by him: "Jump in the Fire," "Phantom Lord," "Metal Militia," and "The Four Horsemen," the last of which was a reworking of "Mechanix." The credits read "Hetfield/Ulrich/Mustaine," but he felt like they had stolen his songs outright.

ABOVE: Jeff Hanneman and Kerry King of Slayer. When they played Judas Priest covers, Hanneman always played K.K. Downing's parts, because they were both blonde. OPPOSITE: Slayer's Kerry King (*foreground*) leads the band (*rear, from left*: Dave Lombardo, Jeff Hanneman, and Tom Araya) as they display their sparkling white teeth and some of their tongues.

"I was out for blood," he said in his memoir. "My goal at the time was to assemble a band, at any cost necessary."

Luckily, a crucial piece of that band lived just downstairs from him. Now living in an apartment complex, he woke up one morning to the sound of amplified bass guitar playing the opening of Van Halen's "Runnin' with the Devil." It was coming from the apartment beneath him, and because he was hungover, the thumping, insistent Michael Anthony bass line might as well have been a jackhammer.

The offending bassist was David Ellefson, who had moved to Los Angeles from a Minnesota farm to break into the music business. After getting to know him and determining that he, too, was an Iron Maiden fan, Mustaine asked Ellefson to join his new band, which was still more of a concept than the bringer of revenge the guitarist envisioned. Since he was younger and also named Dave, the guitarist christened him "Junior." It stuck.

Meanwhile, Slayer was making their record, which they financed themselves. Araya had been working in a hospital as a respiratory therapist and used money he had saved to pay for the recording. In 2006, he told an *ESP Guitars* forum live chat that King's father had also pitched in.

Original Anthrax bassist and cofounder Dan Lilker lays down the low end at L'Amour in September 1983. He left the band in 1984, but this injustice was corrected when he joined ex-bandmates Scott Ian and Charlie Benante in S.O.D. for the immortal *Speak English or Die!* album.

The resulting album, *Show No Mercy*, was released on December 3, 1983. Nobody won a Grammy for the sound quality, but it was raw as hell, and the audience for this music wasn't looking for sparkling production. They were looking for fast tempos and evil imagery. Metallica may have been trying to steer clear of the satanic subject matter they believed to be clichéd, but Slayer went as hard with it as you can go without burning down churches.

In short order, *Show No Mercy* became the biggest-selling Metal Blade release yet. Slagel estimated that it sold somewhere between 15,000 and 20,000 copies, very impressive for an unknown band playing commercially hopeless music. Bernard Doe of *Metal Forces*, who had given their demo a rave review just a few months earlier, was not disappointed.

"One of the heaviest, fastest, most awesome albums of all time," he wrote of the Slayer debut. "Side one contains two satanical mayhem classics—the 100mph opener 'Evil Has No Boundaries' and closer 'Metal Storm / Face the Slayer,' which has a great buildup that explodes into a barrage of metallic death. Sandwiched between these gems are 'The Antichrist,' 'Die by the Sword,' and 'Fight Till Death.' Each guaranteed to give severe neck dislocation to all but the hardest of hardcore metal fans."

He compared the music to that of Metallica, Exciter, and Venom, and gave it a near-perfect 9 out of 10, saying the band played in two modes: "fast and faster." He even said "The Final Command" was "on the verge of being too fast." He wrapped up with kind words for the vocalist and the band in general. "['Black Magic'] is for me the highlight of the album, with bassist Tom Araya's Cronos-like vocals delivering tales of evil amidst a wall of tight riffing, power drumming, and lightning lead work," he said. "This is just fuckin' excellent!!!"

In closing, Doe posed a question that was germane in 1983 and would gain more importance over the next couple of years: "How much heavier and faster can heavy metal get?"

Tom Araya of Slayer, fresh from driving the band from gig to gig in his U-Haul-towing Camaro.

REVIEW

METALLICA

Kill 'Em All

METALLICA'S DEBUT ALBUM was released on July 25, 1983, through Megaforce Records. It was originally going to be called *Metal Up Your Ass* and feature cover art depicting a knife-wielding hand emerging from a toilet bowl, perhaps in tribute to Edmund Ironside. Jon Zazula, believing this might make it hard to sell at Kmart, convinced them to change it. The rest is history.

"Like Motörhead at 78 RPM, it was a defiant blur of an opening statement from a band who would, unbeknownst to anyone at the time, change the face of metal forever," Nick Ruskell wrote of the debut in *Kerrang!* in 2020.

It starts with "Hit the Lights," and Hetfield's voice is better here than on the demo versions, but he's still shout-singing and yet to develop his own approach. The lyrics about kicking ass and metal madness could use an editor, too. It's followed by "The Four Horsemen" (formerly "Mechanix"), and it's impossible to unhear that it's the same song once you've heard the original. It's a bit of a bummer, to be honest.

The Cliff Burton bass showcase "(Anesthesia)—Pulling Teeth" segues into "Whiplash," the song Ulrich said was inspired by Venom. The lyrics are certainly dumb enough, so much so that Hetfield would outsource the second verse to bassist Jason Newsted in live performances because he was ashamed of them.

Side two starts with "Phantom Lord," a seriously underrated song that finds Hetfield occasionally singing in a lower range to great effect. "No Remorse" shows Hammett soloing like crazy right from the beginning, and you can see how he would have passed his audition even if the band hadn't had gigs lined up in five days. He's excellent on "Seek & Destroy," too. Truly, Hammett is wholly undeserving of the scorn he receives from the argumentative comment section edgelords, who prefer Mustaine.

The festivities wrap up with "Metal Militia," which Hulks out right at the beginning with an aggressive, chromatic, and descending riff. You're not whisked along with it so much as dragged behind it. It ends with the sound of marching soldier boots, which is brilliant; whoever thought of that deserved to be the Metallica Employee of the Month. It ends the record in spectacular fashion, and while *Kill 'Em All* is ultimately a little "proto," the newness of it still comes through.

"Each track is guaranteed for 100 percent brain destruction," Bernard Doe wrote in his 10 out of 10 review in *Metal Forces*. "If, when you've heard it, you dislike *Kill 'Em All*, then you can no longer call yourself a heavy metal fan."

TRULY, HAMMETT IS WHOLLY UNDESERVING OF THE SCORN HE RECEIVES FROM THE ARGUMENTATIVE COMMENT SECTION EDGELORDS WHO PREFER MUSTAINE.

REVIEW

SLAYER

Show No Mercy

THE DEBUT SLAYER album was released on December 3, 1983, through Metal Blade Records. It's raw, dark, and murky, but the amateurism in the songwriting and the mix are actually positives—it sounds like crap, but crap whose authenticity can't be questioned.

"Evil Has No Boundaries" kicks off the record with high-speed guitar and an extended shriek from Araya. The band's sound is most of the way there—it just needs more money and less reverb.

Araya cannot sing at all. While that would ruin most records, it makes no difference here, because this album is not about vocal melody—or any melody, for that matter. In fact, Dark Angel drummer Gene Hoglan told *Metal Hammer* in 2024 that Araya had invented a new vocal style on the song "Die by the Sword," so who needs singing? "I think Tom invented the death metal vocal style with the 'watch as flowers decay' line," he said. "Nobody had ever sung that low before. Suddenly, everybody started doing it."

Many critics thought the record was worthless garbage and were happy to say so. Even *Kerrang!*, a rock magazine thought to be friendly to the metal cause, ran a scathing review that described it as "pure, unadulterated junk."

Slagel told *Metal Hammer* in 2024 that *Kerrang!* was not an outlier, either: "The bigger magazines in the UK were not fans."

King agreed with Slagel's assessment. "People hated us," he told *Metal Hammer*. However, he added that being trashed in the media got the band's name out there, which helped them build an audience later on. "Even though we were still getting shitty reviews, people started coming to shows," he said.

Critics from outside of the underground metal scene may have hated the record, but within the scene, it was a different story. Exodus guitarist Gary Holt told *Metal Hammer* that hearing *Show No Mercy* was validating to him and his band, who were making music in the same genre. "We were like, 'These guys are just like us,'" he remembered. "We want to kill shit and hack things up with machetes with them!"

Joe Daly put *Show No Mercy* into historical perspective in *Metal Hammer* in 2023. He said it represented the moment when Slayer separated from the pack and began to lead the way. "[It] detonated with the force of a concussion grenade, clearing the way for its genre's fiery evolution," he said. "At a time when the parameters of fast-paced metal were still being defined, Slayer screamed a seismic war cry that echoed across the globe."

Decades after its release, it's easy to see the ripple effect the album had. But in 1984, K. J. Doughton of *Metal Forces* was not thinking about the record's future impact because he was too immersed in the thirty-five minutes comprising *Show No Mercy*. "Every cut exceeds the 100mph mark, with not a melody or vocal harmony within earshot," he wrote. "Just an onslaught of pure, unadulterated, wonderful noise!"

"PEOPLE HATED US," KING TOLD METAL HAMMER. HOWEVER, HE ADDED THAT BEING TRASHED IN THE MEDIA GOT THE BAND'S NAME OUT THERE.

Dan Spitz and Neil Turbin of Anthrax lay waste to L'Amour in Brooklyn in February 1984.

CHAPTER 4

1984: CHEMICAL WARFARE

ABOVE: Kerry King and Jeff Hanneman of Slayer (correct spelling: SLAAAAAYERRRRRRR!!!!!!) at the now sadly defunct Spectrum in Montreal on October 29, 1984.
OPPOSITE: Metallica's Lars Ulrich and James Hetfield, giddy and twitterpated with thrash-metal glee on the Aardschok Festival stage in 1984.

Slayer played their first gig of 1984 on January 2 in Berkeley, California, and their last on New Year's Eve in San Francisco. It was the year they played their first North American club tour, which included three gigs at L'Amour, the site of Mustaine's final Metallica show. Scott Ian told *Kerrang!* in 2018 that he was present at one of those dates with his brother Jason, who got his nose broken in the pit. Even back then, Slayer pits were not for the squeamish, but Ian's little brother responded correctly to the injury.

"He actually left the pit, wiped the blood off, and jumped right back in," the guitarist said.

Slayer got from gig to gig in Araya's Camaro, which had a U-Haul trailer hitched to it. He said they booked the tour themselves, using a bunch of phone numbers and addresses supplied to them by Slagel. There was no crew, no road manager, and scant money to keep the band fed. Araya told *Decibel* in 2006 that was partially due to the band's inexperience. "We didn't realize that you had to ask for money up front," he said.

Nevertheless, they plowed through. Hanneman said they survived by channeling what money they could get into "beer, food, and gas."

Slayer's 1984 tour apparatus could politely be described as "barely acceptable," and one could say the same for most of the venues on their itinerary. Some were in alarming states of disrepair, such as Boston's Lizard Lounge. "A car had run into the front of the building, and it was all boarded up," Araya said. "We still played there."

Metallica's 1984 visit to Boston was worse. They were playing at the Channel on January 22, 1984, just before they were about to embark on their first European tour, and all of their equipment was stolen. That included Hetfield's prized Marshall amplifier, which had a unique tone that was next to impossible to replicate.

Luckily, there would be an unexpected upside to the theft of his beloved gear. The despair inspired him to write "Fade to Black," an all-time classic that the band still performs to this day.

Metal Forces valued the equipment at $40,000. A lot of bands with less pluck would have postponed their tour. Others would have canceled it, while others still would have just broken up in the face of that loss. Luckily, Hetfield said Ulrich is "100 percent Metallica all the time," and giving up was not in his blood.

Instead, the drummer flew to London ahead of the band and arranged to rent equipment for a scheduled European tour. According to *Metal Injection*, Metallica's Megaforce label mates, Anthrax, loaned them equipment as well. The all-hands-on-deck response to the theft allowed the tour to begin as scheduled on February 3 in Zürich.

Meanwhile, Anthrax was having existential issues of its own. Ian said singer Neil Turbin had unilaterally fired bassist and cofounder Lilker for being "a slob." The timing had the band over a barrel, since they had a tour booked and felt they couldn't let that opportunity pass them by. They had to suck it up.

"Scott was put very much between a rock and a hard place," Lilker told *Ultimate Guitar* in 2024. "I got over that and formed Nuclear Assault . . . I'm not the kind of guy who stays bitter forever."

Anthrax had to stay on track for another reason besides the tour. The thrash scene was turning into something, and while it was still an underground movement, more people were coming to gigs. It felt like word was slowly but visibly getting out.

Somehow in the middle of all this, King began splitting his time between Slayer and the newly formed Megadeth, which hadn't finalized a lineup. The association didn't last long, just five gigs and a couple of months, but the performances with King on second guitar helped Megadeth start to gain notice.

LEFT: Jeff Hanneman of Slayer, the Big Four's most fearsome foursome. They held the title of most diabolical band on Earth until the Scandinavian black metallers came along. RIGHT: Dave Lombardo of Slayer showing every aspiring drummer on earth how it's supposed to be done. He was in and out of the band more than once, but damn . . . the guy could play his ass off.

Ellefson said in his 2013 memoir, *My Life with Deth*, that the band had been looking for a guitarist at Mustaine's level. Few were up to the challenge, but King was able to keep pace. "Kerry was the only one who came in and nailed the music right away," he said. "Dave showed him some riffs—really complex stuff—and Kerry instantly mirrored it and played it right back at him, note for note."

King returned to Slayer, but by then, Megadeth's lineup had started piecing itself together. Drummer Gar Samuelson had joined, and his jazz background gave his playing a distinct flavor that drummers raised on Phil Rudd didn't have.

Mustaine said Samuelson was a heroin user, something he learned when the drummer auditioned. The guitarist described him as "completely strung out on dope," but once he started playing, concern for that evaporated. "Within just a few seconds, I knew he was the right guy," the guitarist said.

Samuelson had played with a guitarist named Chris Poland, whom he brought into the band. Poland also had a jazz background and his chemistry with the drummer was immediately apparent. When he joined, Megadeth finally had a real lineup, and it was explosive.

Drug use, however, would prove a persistent problem. The guitarist said sometimes when he came to rehearsal, the drum kit was without cymbals because Samuelson had pawned them to buy heroin. This happened more than once, and before long, heroin would prove to be an issue for the entire band.

Mustaine was laser-focused on Megadeth's music, which had its own distinct identity and sound. Some people may have expected him to emerge with something like Diet Metallica, but he was crafting something else entirely with the intention of making Metallica sound like Barry Manilow.

As he plotted revenge against his old band, they were about to take a major step forward, one that would have implications for the entire thrash genre. It would even have positive implications for Megadeth. After an August 3, 1984, concert at New York City's Roseland Ballroom, Metallica signed to Elektra Records, a major label.

Metallica had gone from the epitome of underground to labelmates with Linda Ronstadt. A&R rep Michael Alago was responsible, and he described seeing them that night in his 2020 memoir, *I Am Michael Alago: Breathing Music. Signing Metallica. Beating Death.*

"The sound was loud, raw, and crushing," he wrote. "When the show ended, the crowd was still insane, screaming madly, banging into each other, crushing and stomping on the balcony, I thought the ceiling rafters would crash down on us. . . . We never wanted Metallica to leave the stage."

Ulrich told *Metal Forces* in 1984 that because of that one night, they won not only a major label deal but also new management and a new booking agency. Despite Alago's description of the gig as triumphant, the drummer recalled the band saw it a little differently. "As soon as we got offstage, we all agreed that it was probably one of the worst gigs we'd ever done," the drummer said.

Fortunately, the decision to pick up Metallica had not come down to just this one gig. Their new management organization, Q Prime, was hitching its wagon to a nascent movement they believed would be huge once it escaped from the underground into mainstream channels.

"Cliff Burnstein, who signed us to our new management deal in the States, has this big belief that what we are doing will be the next big thing in heavy metal," Ulrich said. "This whole Ratt, Mötley Crüe, Quiet Riot, Black 'N Blue thing will get kinda old and die out. . . . Metallica will lead the way in a sort of new 'true metal' trend."

Predictably, some of their earliest fans expressed skepticism about Metallica affiliating themselves with a major label. The drummer knew that because those fans put it in writing and mailed it to them. "We even got letters from fans who asked Metallica not to get big because it would take the fun out of liking us," he said.

ABOVE: A photocopied flyer advertising an in-store appearance by Slayer at the legendary New York City record store It's Only Rock 'n' Roll. This era was as glorious as it was low rent. RIGHT: A flyer advertising the 1984 New York City concert that got Metallica signed to Elektra Records. It was also the final show of Neil Turbin's tenure with Anthrax.

Elektra bought out Metallica's contract with Megaforce Records, eventually reissuing *Kill 'Em All* and *Ride the Lightning*, the latter of which was only a couple of months old. August 3 had been a pivotal night for them, and it proved pivotal to Anthrax as well. They were on the same bill and it was the last date of their tour with Metallica and Raven. With that out of the way, they fired their vocalist, who was very much on the outs with them by that point.

Years later, when Ian's memoir was released, Turbin said his depiction in the book was wholly fictional. He didn't name names or get specific about any incidents, but he took to his blog, *Deathriders*, to call shenanigans on the way Ian had characterized him. "I find it very sad that somebody I've had no contact [with] for thirty years feels that it's necessary to fabricate lies about me in order to draw attention to themselves," the singer wrote. He never used Ian's name or even gave the name of the book in which he felt he had been smeared, but he denied all of Ian's allegations.

In any event, Anthrax was now without a singer and had studio time coming up. *Fistful of Metal* producer Carl Canedy knew one from upstate New York named Joey Belladonna and connected him with the band. The vocalist was blissfully unaware of the band and its genre.

"I had no clue," Belladonna told *Metal Hammer* in 2021. "I'd never heard of them."

Belladonna was a dyed-in-the-wool rock guy, something he proved at the audition when he sang Foreigner's "Hot Blooded." He dressed the part, too.

"In walks this guy who looks like he should be in Whitesnake," Ian said.

Despite the possible clash of styles, Ian and Benante both said they couldn't deny his singing.

"When Joey came into the band, it was right," the drummer said. "It just sounded like, that's it, that's the band right there, don't touch it."

ABOVE: James Hetfield and Kirk Hammett bring thrash metal to the Aardschok stage on February 11, 1984, when there were still precious few other bands doing it. LEFT: Megadeth (*from left*: Chris Poland, Dave Mustaine, Gar Samuelson, and David Ellefson) on December 28, 1984, at L'Amour in Brooklyn. The last time Mustaine played there, he was subsequently kicked out of Metallica, so it was a good place to play on his revenge tour. OPPOSITE: James Hetfield and Kirk Hammett in a Flying V frenzy.

ABOVE: Scott Ian and Frank Bello of Anthrax at Brooklyn's L'Amour in February 1984. Fun fact: Bello is drummer Charlie Benante's nephew. OPPOSITE TOP: Anthrax (*from left*: Neil Turbin, Dan Spitz, and Scott Ian) in February 1984. Say what you want about Turbin, but how many people can say they perform Halford-esque lead vocals on a record whose cover features a guy with two right hands? OPPOSITE BOTTOM: Anthrax (*from left*: Dan Spitz, Frank Bello, and Scott Ian) in February 1984. Bello was brought into the band to replace cofounder Dan Lilker after his less-than-ideal ejection.

It took a little time for Belladonna to educate himself about thrash and find a way to sing over it that worked with the music. Eventually, it clicked.

"He caught on quickly, and once he learned something, he made it his own and sang the shit out of it," the guitarist said.

Megadeth was also making strides. Their *Last Rites* demo had made the rounds with tape traders, eventually catching the attention of record companies. They had no luck with the majors, so they signed with an indie, Combat Records, who gave them $8,000 to make their first album. That was not a lot of money to do the job, even in 1984.

There was another issue, and it went deeper than having a minimal budget. Ellefson said that when the band entered the studio to make their debut, every member of the group was using heroin, including himself. It wasn't recreational, either. That being the case, half the recording budget got spent on drugs, leaving the band to go back to Combat for another $4,000 to finish it.

Ellefson noted that the eight songs they recorded were taken at much faster tempos than originally intended. He laid this at the feet of a single fan letter, which expressed the hope that Megadeth's songs would be faster than Metallica's. The bassist said Mustaine simply couldn't resist.

"The next day we sped up all the songs by about forty beats per minute," Ellefson said. "That one fan letter changed Megadeth's sound overnight."

WANTED
BIKERS
PIT
Marshall

Marshall
Marshall

ABOVE: Kerry King and Tom Arayain front of the already legendary Slayer crowd.
LEFT: Jeff Hanneman, who wrote "Angel of Death," the song that would become Slayer's "More Than a Feeling."

Metallica's James Hetfield and Kirk Hammett at Roseland Ballroom in New York City on August 3, 1984. Ulrich said they didn't like the performance that night, but they still got signed to Elektra.

ABOVE: James Hetfield and Kirk Hammett bring epic down-picking fury to the European continent on February 11, 1984, at Aardschok. OPPOSITE: The mighty Cliff Burton in his most famous pose—low-slung bass, foot on the monitor, and bell-bottom jeans, which were not easy to find in 1984.

THE LYRICS TO "ANTHRAX" ARE ROCK-STUPID AND EMBODY EVERY CLICHÉ PEOPLE CITE AS REASONS THEY HATE HEAVY METAL.

REVIEW

ANTHRAX

Fistful of Metal

THE DEBUT ANTHRAX album was released on January 6, 1984, through Megaforce Records. It was the only Anthrax record to feature the services of bassist Dan Lilker and singer Neil Turbin, the latter of whom is unambiguous throughout about his Rob Halford fandom.

When he opens "Metal Thrashing Mad" with a sustained shriek, it plainly recalls "Stained Class," with perhaps a *soupçon* of Paul Stanley thrown in. His midrange voice is solid, and musically, he doesn't do anything objectionable. The primary complaint is the copious abundance of those Halford shrieks. Indeed, they are so prodigious, one wonders whether he isn't contractually obligated to produce at least seven within a thirty-five-minute period.

Charlie Benante, Scott Ian, and Lilker are tight as hell and carry the entire record. Their collective sound is that of a piece of heavy machinery, come to life and programmed to maim.

Nevertheless, there's a cover of Alice Cooper's "I'm Eighteen" that simply doesn't belong on the record. At all. Jon Zazula wanted Anthrax to follow the example set by Quiet Riot with their chart-topping cover of Slade's "Cum on Feel the Noize," and while it's highly unlikely that he thought Anthrax would hit number one because they had covered a song, too, it just doesn't work. Ian was so opposed to recording it, he refused to play on the track.

While "I'm Eighteen" is all wrong for the record, it's not the worst thing on it. "Anthrax" and "Howling Furies" are neck-and-neck for that distinction, and it's a photo finish.

The lyrics to "Anthrax" are rock-stupid and embody every cliché people cite as reasons they hate heavy metal. It's their "Lady Evil." "Howling Furies," meanwhile, is just a wet firecracker. It's preceded by the brief instrumental, "Across the River," apparently a vehicle for Dan Spitz's lead guitar genius, but no matter how much he hammers away, he adds nothing. He sounds like he's practicing and someone just happened to record it.

Fistful of Metal also has the distinction of being graced by one of the dumbest album covers ever made, depicting a guy getting punched through his head and out of his mouth by an unseen assailant. Furthermore, close inspection reveals that the assailant's fist and the hand grabbing his victim's hair are both the right hands.

In 2024, Joe Daly of *Metal Hammer* said that of Anthrax's eleven studio albums, *Fistful of Metal* was number eleven. He didn't hate on it, but he wasn't wrong when he said it was "the band's weakest and most erratic effort."

Ian still stands behind *Fistful of Metal* today, though not all of it—he has been vocal about his disdain for both the mix and the cover's implication that there are people walking around out there with two right hands. But there was one area in which he felt *Fistful of Metal* got it right, and it's the only one that really counts: "Everything was wrong with the album except the music," he said.

REVIEW

SLAYER

Haunting the Chapel

SHOW NO MERCY was Metal Blade's highest seller yet, so Slagel sent Slayer back to the studio to strike while the iron was hot. The resulting EP was released on August 4, 1984, and Dark Angel drummer Gene Hoglan noted a preoccupation with the devil permeating its lyrics: "Boy, they were praising some Satan with that one," he said.

It opens with "Chemical Warfare," and one is immediately struck by the fact that the band has somehow become even faster in the nine months since their last release. K. J. Doughton said as much in his 1984 review in *Metal Forces*: "Slayer are bound and determined to do nothing but push the boundaries of death metal beyond the sound barrier," he wrote. "Such cuts as the gloriously fast 'Chemical Warfare' [set] a new standard in audio-brain impalement."

It's followed by "Captor of Sin," which has no thrash section. The whole point of the EP is to get to the thrash section. That's why people bought it.

Some may disagree, but there are no audible improvements to the mix to discuss here—it remains as mired in toxic mud as the debut. In fact, one wonders how they knew they were done mixing it.

Whatever its deficiencies, *Haunting the Chapel* does the job. The speed and aggression are undeniable, and in its thirteen and a half minutes, one gets the sense that these guys were out to offend with their sound alone, and they absolutely succeeded. There are no words in the English language that stand a chance of offending people as much as this music will.

"SLAYER ARE BOUND AND DETERMINED TO DO NOTHING BUT PUSH THE BOUNDARIES OF DEATH METAL BEYOND THE SOUND BARRIER."

—K. J. Doughton, *Metal Forces*

REVIEW

METALLICA

Ride the Lightning

METALLICA'S SECOND ALBUM was released on July 27, 1984. The liner notes indicate that it was produced by Metallica and assisted by Flemming Rasmussen and Mark Whitaker, which is quite a mouthful. However, while it doesn't indicate who twiddled which knob when, the proof is in the pudding. The album is a massive leap forward in terms of songwriting, performance, and sound quality.

The record connected with fans on a deeper level than previously thought possible for thrash metal, largely due to the song "Fade to Black." It may have been written only because some asshole stole Hetfield's amp, but he converted that experience into a song that many people will tell you saved their lives. It penetrated the fog of their depression and mirrored what they felt, and there's nothing on *Kill 'Em All* you can say that about.

The record opens with "Fight Fire with Fire." They're out for blood and out to innovate, as epitomized by the few measures of unaccompanied double bass after the guitar solo—that sound was revelatory during the Huey Lewis years, and the repeated "fight fire with fire" at the end of the vocals is just sick. It ends with a nuclear bomb detonating, and that's just the first song.

It segues directly into the title track, in which Hetfield's downpicking is truly menacing. He gets certain guitar overtones that sound almost motorized, and his singing is much better. When he sings "they're trying to take it all away," it could almost be called a hook.

The midtempo solo section, while remaining totally metal, has an operatic melancholy to it. The band develops that and expands upon it when the tempo accelerates during the guitar solo and Hammett plays arpeggios over a descending riff. It demonstrates that Metallica connected as well as they did with audiences because no matter what they were doing, they never forgot to put music in their music.

"For Whom the Bell Tolls" features an overdriven melody line by Burton that many people probably didn't know was a bass upon first hearing it. Then we get a palm-muted chromatic riff that's so intimidating it feels like the listener is in imminent physical danger.

The record loses steam on side two. "Trapped Under Ice" and "Escape" are perfectly serviceable songs, but neither approaches the quality of what's on side one. "Creeping Death" then comes along and redeems side two in its entirety, right from its insistent opening. It tells the story of Passover, so when you invite the band over for your next Seder, make sure you have enough yarmulkes for everybody.

The album closes with the nine-minute instrumental, "The Call of Ktulu," which would be much better as a three-minute instrumental. Metallica could get long in the tooth, often to their detriment. However, it didn't matter. Whatever its weaknesses, *Ride the Lightning* makes the band's point, and everyone heard it loud and clear.

"Upon its release, it was clear the goalposts had shifted," Nick Ruskell said in *Kerrang!* in 2020. "It set a precedent for Metallica remaining, not one step ahead, but on a different route entirely from their peers. It announced that they were different, as well as throwing down the gauntlet to everyone else to pull their socks up."

WHATEVER ITS WEAKNESSES, RIDE THE LIGHTNING MAKES THE BAND'S POINT, AND EVERYONE HEARD IT LOUD AND CLEAR.

REVIEW

SLAYER

Live Undead

SLAYER RELEASED *LIVE UNDEAD* on November 16, 1984. It would be great to say it was recorded in a nightclub packed with hundreds of lunatics, all drunk on thrash metal rage, but it ain't so. It was recorded at Tiki Recording Studios in Glen Cove, New York, and the "audience" size remains a matter of hot debate. Was it ten or was it twelve?

Whatever the number, it didn't consist of paying customers. They were there to provide the illusion that this was a nightclub performance, which it wasn't, and at no time does it sound like one.

The good news is that it's the best-sounding thing Slayer had released so far. "Black Magic," "The Antichrist," and "Evil Has No Boundaries" all sound noticeably better than their studio counterparts, making these versions definitive if you can ignore the sound of ten people yelling in response to nothing in particular.

The record peaks early, courtesy of the vocalist. When Araya announces that "Die by the Sword" is up next, he adds, "They say the pen is mightier than the sword . . . well, I say, fuck the pen!"

He has other, similarly inappropriate things to say at the beginning of "Captor of Sin." Honestly, the between-song banter is an absolute highlight of this record.

Live Undead is the earliest Slayer record where you can really hear what Lombardo is playing, which is welcome. The "audience" chanting SLAYER out of time with the music, as they do during "Show No Mercy," is not welcome. You never buy into the concept that this is a live record, so no illusions are destroyed, but it affords a very distracting glimpse of the man behind the curtain. Buy it for the improved production and between-song banter. Ignore everything else.

LIVE UNDEAD WAS RECORDED AT TIKI RECORDING STUDIOS IN GLEN COVE, NEW YORK, AND THE "AUDIENCE" SIZE REMAINS A MATTER OF HOT DEBATE. WAS IT TEN OR WAS IT TWELVE?

Slayer's Kerry King, the man who coauthored the moonstruck romantic ballad "Necrophiliac," offers a friendly *begroeting* to Eindhoven's Dynamo Festival on May 28, 1985.

CHAPTER 5

1985: BUSINESS IS GOOD

Devil's grip, iron fist. Scott Ian of Anthrax in 1985 at the band's home away from home, L'Amour in Brooklyn.

Elektra Records recording artists Metallica started 1985 on tour with W.A.S.P. and Armored Saint. Kansas City radio personality Johnny Dare was at the February 19 gig at the Uptown Theater and described the scene to *Ultimate Metallica*: "Metallica gets up there," he said. "They play faster and harder than anyone we had ever heard, but they all looked like the road crew who just set their shit up . . . you were seeing something completely different than anything the eighties had given you when you saw Metallica."

Brian McTavish was less favorable two days later. He slated them in a *Kansas City Times* review whose headline should have been, "I Don't Get It": "James Hetfield seemed to have as much fun screaming obscenities at those crammed on the floor in front of the stage as he did dotting songs with throaty explosions that would have ruined any accomplished singer's voice," he wrote.

He would have been no happier watching Anthrax. They were playing a series of East Coast dates to break in their new singer, who had never attended a thrash metal gig in his life. They rented an RV, driven by Psychos bassist Billy Milano, and took Joey Belladonna on a tour of some of the most savage crowds in America.

"There was blood, there was chaos," Scott Ian said. "Joey loved it."

Other changes were underway. Charlie Benante told *JAM* in 2013 that he had taken on a larger role in Anthrax as a songwriter. "I wrote more of the music, while Scott wrote more of the lyrics,' the drummer said. "The other guys in the band also contributed, but I would usually come in with the basic framework of each song."

Dan Spitz told *Metal Forces* in 1985 about the change the band had made at the microphone. He briefly mentioned "personal differences" with Neil Turbin before moving on to praise the guy who had replaced him. "He's the Steve Perry of aggressive metal," the guitarist said. "When we first heard him in the studio, he just blew our heads apart, and he's been a brother ever since."

With Belladonna more integrated into the band, it was time to go back to the studio and finish off their next album, *Spreading the Disease*. Slayer, meanwhile, was with Exodus and Venom on the *North American Combat* tour. Exodus guitarist Gary Holt told *Decibel* in 2006 that the two California bands hit it off right away. "We immediately bonded with the Slayer guys," he said. "It was two bands of friends playing with one band of heroes, you know?"

The tour hit numerous cities, including New York, where the bands brought thrash metal to the disco capital of the world,

Studio 54. Lombardo said that on Venom's tour bus Araya gave that legendary venue a run for its money in the debauchery department. The drummer was in the back with Venom front man Cronos when a quite inebriated Araya announced his need to go tinkle. As a joke, Cronos told him to do it in his mouth. "[Tom] whipped it out and went to the bathroom on Cronos's hair," Lombardo said. "Cronos got up, grabbed Tom, and punched him in the face . . . Tom did the rest of the tour with a black eye."

Another stop was in San Francisco, which Lombardo rightly described to *Metal Hammer* in 2023 as "the thrash metal epicenter." It was Exodus's turf, and the hometown crowd gave that band a hero's welcome. "People were climbing up the speakers and leaping off," he said. "One time, a kid tried to jump off the balcony onto the stage but landed feet-first and went through the stage, so his torso was sticking out, trying to wiggle out."

Amid all the flying urine and protruding torsos, Slayer released their next record, *Hell Awaits*, on April 8. They barely had a moment to catch their breath before they were back at it in May, this time embarking on their first European tour.

It started at the Heavy Sound Festival in Belgium, followed by numerous dates in the Netherlands, including one at a Katwijk venue known as SCUM CLUB. There were also dates with those titanic Teutonic terrors, Destruction.

The final date of the tour was on June 24 at London's Marquee Club. They played fifteen songs off a set list written on a pizza take-out box; the official Slayer site claims that the venue banned thrash gigs due to the resulting pandemonium.

"We'd never seen anything as intense as that," said attendee Marty Rigby on the official Slayer website. "I remember thinking that sort of gig, you're not going to get many of these in your lifetime . . . the crowd—it was crazy."

Back in the States, Megadeth had released their debut album, *Killing Is My Business . . . and Business Is Good!* Finishing it had proved challenging, and not just because they'd had to go back to Combat to ask for more money. Dave Mustaine told *Metal Forces* in 1985 that they had also fired the producer, Jay Jones, in the middle of the sessions. "It wasn't turning out right," the guitarist said. "We just took over and produced the album ourselves."

The album's title is inspired by the titular character in the comic book *The Punisher*, and it was supposed to have a cool cover to go with it. The guitarist had created sketches of the band's mascot, Vic Rattlehead: a skeleton with sunglasses bolted to his face, his mouth clamped shut, and his ears blocked. It was meant to embody the proverb "See no evil, hear no evil, speak no evil" in a commentary about censorship. Very metal.

Elektra Records recording artists Metallica, fully in the zone at Brooklyn's L'Amour.

Metallica and Venom at the Breaking Sound Festival on August 29, 1984, at La Rotonde in Le Bourget, France. *From left*: Mantas, Kirk Hammett, Cronos, Lars Ulrich, and Abaddon.

The guitarist said the label lost his sketches and decided to wing it themselves. They created a plastic skull with sunglasses and metal hooks wiring its jaw shut. It looked like you could open it and find candy inside. Not metal.

It would take a lot more than that to make Mustaine go off mission. He had a dish best served cold that he still needed to give his old band. "The reason that I wanted to keep soldiering on was revenge," he said.

Less than three weeks after the release of *Killing Is My Business . . .*, Anthrax finished mixing *Spreading the Disease.* They left the instruments and microphones set up because Ian and Benante were about to make another record, and it would not be for Anthrax.

Ian had been drawing cartoon strips depicting a right-wing, cigar-chomping zombie named Sgt. D, and he wanted to combine it with hardcore music. This resulted in a band called Stormtroopers of Death, or S.O.D., and Ian enlisted Anthrax cofounder Dan Lilker. The microphone duties were handled by Billy Milano.

Anthrax finished mixing *Spreading the Disease* on June 30. S.O.D. had a single day of rehearsal on July 1. The album was tracked the next day, and Milano's vocals were recorded the day after that. It was mixed on July 5 and dubbed *Speak English or Die.*

The mighty Cliff Burton of Metallica in Royal Oak, Michigan, on February 1, 1985, doing the thing he loved the most—giving the Misfits free advertising.

S.O.D. played seven dates to promote it, one at L'Amour. An audience member was spitting at them, so Milano responded by pulling him out of the audience, pummeling him bloody, and breaking his arm. "Billy got his point across," Ian said. "Don't fucking spit on us."

Metallica was also dodging projectiles, but in a different country. In 2014, Ulrich told the *Guardian* that during their performance at Monsters of Rock at Castle Donington on August 17, an audience member threw a pig's head onstage.

Two weeks later, on August 31, was the Day on the Green in Oakland. Their performance was filmed for MTV, much of it from Burton's side of the stage. He spends his screentime upending the popular perception of the bass as a background instrument.

"Cliff stands at the forefront in what has become an iconic picture of him; wearing his denim jacket, black Misfits T-shirt, and bell-bottom jeans," Brandon Oberkrieser of the *Metallicast* podcast said in *Metal Talk* in 2020. "He is standing with one foot up on the PA speakers, his mane of hair covering his face as he headbangs."

Appearing on MTV gave Metallica their widest exposure yet, and by this point, there was no denying their increased visibility had paved the way for thrash metal to gain more mainstream acceptance. Megadeth had signed to Capitol, Anthrax had worldwide distribution through Island Records, and even the determinedly uncommercial Slayer was attracting label interest.

The label that courted them was Def Jam, which only had rap artists on its roster. It also had distribution through Columbia Records. Most importantly, though, it wasn't a matter of a label signing some thrash band because the music was getting popular. Hanneman told *Decibel* in 2006 that label cofounder Rick Rubin was genuinely enthusiastic about Slayer and wanted to present them as they truly were. "I loved what we were doing, but I figured nobody else would get it," he said. "Rubin totally got it, though."

ABOVE: Scott Ian of Anthrax in August 1985 (*background, from left*: Frank Bello, Dan Spitz). The band's fortunes had improved a bit, so they graduated from playing tiny shitholes to playing New York City's legendary Ritz, a more spacious shithole. RIGHT: What has two thumbs and sings for Anthrax? Joey Belladonna, who got the gig in 1985 after the band and Neil Turbin consciously uncoupled.

Metallica (*from left*: Kirk Hammett, James Hetfield, Lars Ulrich, and Cliff Burton) at a time in their career when they looked almost indistinguishable from their fans.

The producer understood that the fans identified with Slayer's music in a way polite society would never be able to. Maybe their teachers and parents didn't understand them, but the California foursome sure did. They even looked like they could have been in the crowd at their own gigs.

"I'd go to a concert and see an arena full of kids who were very much like the guys in Slayer, who were so filled with joy listening to this music," Rubin told *Metal Hammer* in 2024. "It was speaking directly to them. It completely was nourishing them."

With Slayer's signing to Def Jam, all the Big Four bands had secured major label deals or distribution. Only a couple of years earlier, that idea was laughable.

After finishing their third album, Metallica played a New Year's Eve gig at the Civic Auditorium in San Francisco. An audience of 6,000 also saw Exodus, Metal Church, and Megadeth. Hetfield and Ulrich had extended the invitation to Mustaine's band after Anthrax backed out. However awkward that load-in might have been, Ron Quintana said in the 2016 book *Metallica: Back to the Front* that once the music started, everything else was drowned out by a surge of bloody, sweaty, chaotic euphoria. Metallica was at a peak, and he couldn't imagine them exceeding it.

"No one realized it was just the start," he said.

RIGHT: Tom Araya of Slayer plucks away at his A string while onlookers throw the horns his way. OPPOSITE: Dave Mustaine of Megadeth sings about one of many possible grievances and traumas he sustained at the hands of his former bandmates.

REVIEW

SLAYER

Hell Awaits

IF REVERB WERE nuclear power, *Hell Awaits* could light every major city in the Western Hemisphere. It was released on April 8, 1985, through Metal Blade Records, which apparently got a deal on studio-generated echo sounds the month it was recorded. It was likely all in the name of sounding like Venom, but it didn't do the record any favors.

It opens with the title track, whose intro is slow and plodding, taking up nearly half of the song. When it speeds up, it's hard not to ask why they didn't just start there and lose the first three minutes entirely.

The record has a lot of "hooks," none of them melodic. They all come from the rhythm guitars, which somehow always seem to find expressive motifs hidden away in those chromatic chord progressions. The solos, meanwhile, are incoherent to the point where Hanneman and King sound blindfolded.

Side two gets right down to business with "Praise of Death," followed by "Necrophiliac," both of which feature stellar performances from Lombardo. If you had to ask where his reputation as one of the greatest heavy metal drummers of all time started, it's right here. If this were a movie, he would be said to be stealing every scene.

"Crypts of Eternity" is an absolute mess. The song is pointlessly long at over six minutes and it's at this point that the listener realizes they're not here for the breakdowns, buildups, and intros. They're here for the blindingly fast 200bpm parts, and everything that isn't that starts to seem like filler.

Someone watching an adult film can probably relate. Patrons of that art form are there to see full-on smut and nothing else. They are not there to see the lonely housewife tell the pizza boy that she has no money. "Crypts of Eternity" is basically an adult film that consists entirely of character development.

The festivities end with "Hardening of the Arteries." Once again, no disrespect to the other guys, but the trophy goes to Lombardo. This is where he became the drummer everyone wanted to air-drum to, assuming they could keep up, and his performance is consistently the reason to revisit this record.

Hell Awaits is a mixed bag comprising inspired playing and patience-trying arrangements in equal measure. Some of it is brilliant, and some of it requires real effort to sit through. They would do significantly better on all fronts next time out.

"CRYPTS OF ETERNITY" IS AN ABSOLUTE MESS. THE SONG IS POINTLESSLY LONG AT OVER SIX MINUTES, AND THE LISTENER'S NOT HERE FOR THE BREAKDOWNS, BUILDUPS, AND INTROS. THEY'RE HERE FOR THE BLINDINGLY FAST 200BPM PARTS.

REVIEW

MEGADETH

Killing Is My Business . . . and Business Is Good!

DAVE MUSTAINE'S revenge tour began on June 12, 1985, with the release of Megadeth's debut album, *Killing Is My Business . . . and Business Is Good!* He had a lot to prove and a massive chip on his shoulder, and while the album's release didn't destroy Metallica's career as he might have hoped, it nonetheless announced Megadeth as a formidable force.

"Last Rites / Loved to Deth" has a Bach-inspired intro featuring piano, which sets them apart from the other Big Four bands in the first thirty seconds. "Loved to Deth" has a filthy, nasty riff, and Mustaine's lead guitar playing is so good you can see how it might have been a dilemma for the Metallica guys to get rid of him.

The title track opens with a riff recalling early ZZ Top before a furious lockstep thrash section sweeps it all away. There are a lot of changes and transitions, and it's as though Mustaine spent the previous two years stockpiling ferocious riffs. Also, there are so many leads, some of them take place while he's singing.

Let's get something out of the way right now. "Mechanix" is superior to "The Four Horsemen." By a lot. The lyrics are incredibly stupid, but the arrangement and insistence on taking the song at a higher tempo sideline that concern.

In 1985, *Metal Forces* asked Mustaine why he had revisited the track, and boy, oh, boy did he ever have an answer-slash-diatribe locked and loaded. "That was just to straighten Metallica up," he said. "They're saying I'm a drunk and I can't play. It's real funny how Kirk Hammett ripped off every lead break I'd played on that *No Life 'til Leather* tape and got voted number-one guitarist in your magazine. . . . God knows when they're gonna stop writing the songs that I originally wrote."

The album wraps up with "These Boots," a cover of Nancy Sinatra's 1965 hit, "These Boots Are Made for Walkin'." Apart from the guitar replicating the descending bass figure from the original's intro, this is a throwaway that's only there because Mustaine likes songs about people getting comeuppance, for some mysterious reason that maybe he'll articulate someday.

Mustaine is the clear ringleader here, but the entire band should be commended for putting something highly original out there. Samuelson's drumming throughout is exceptional; he played a significant role in the originality of their sound and it's a shame he made only one more record with them.

WHILE THE ALBUM'S RELEASE DIDN'T DESTROY METALLICA'S CAREER AS MUSTAINE MIGHT HAVE HOPED, IT NONETHELESS ANNOUNCED MEGADETH AS A FORMIDABLE FORCE.

REVIEW

S.O.D.

Speak English or Die

RELEASED ON AUGUST 30, 1985, *Speak English or Die* was intended as a side project but accidentally became one of the most important thrash metal records ever made. Thus, while S.O.D. is not technically part of the Big Four, this record is being grandfathered in—it goes a long way toward making up for how Lilker's time in Anthrax ended, which was worse than how *Lost* ended.

The songs are taken at D.R.I. tempos (translation: very fast), and vocalist Billy Milano does not attempt to sing for one second. He just yells like Tony Soprano, which is exactly the right approach to these songs.

The lyrics to the title track are fully out of compliance with modern-day wokeness requirements. In 1985, Ian told *Metal Forces* that lyrics like "Nice fuckin' accent, why can't you speak like me" were not meant to be jingoistic—it was just a fun take on life in the Big Apple, whose ethnically diverse population can sometimes get into hilarious misunderstandings thanks to the language barrier.

Some songs should never have been recorded, many of them lasting less than ten seconds. They're barely amusing the first time you hear them, and you will absolutely hate them if subjected to them a second time. "What's That Noise," for example, constitutes the longest minute in human history.

Ian defended the practice of making really short, annoying songs with no purpose. In fact, he said that six-second "The Ballad of Jimi Hendrix" was one of the band's most popular selections in a concert setting, with attendees yelling for them to play it again and again. "When we do that live, we end up doing it five times in a row," he said.

Overall, the hits outnumber the misses, and the blinding speed is a marvel to behold. "Kill Yourself" features no transitions into the fast bits, just four drumstick clicks at a tempo too fast to identify and they're off. Lilker's bass propels the whole thing forward with a blur so fast it cannot be measured with musical notation. "Pussy Whipped," "Fist Banging Mania," and "Douche Crew" are all immortal classics as well, and that last one has a breakdown riff with an almost Middle Eastern tinge.

Speaking of which, the record features "Fuck the Middle East," which at thirty seconds long is no less than the Michelangelo's *David* of politically incorrect songs. Some might find the lyrics insensitive to the plight of those living in the war-torn region. In 2011, Ian told *Tablet* that its citizens had only themselves to blame for that. If they had but taken the Queens crossover band's sage wisdom to heart, maybe the world would be a different place. "They should've listened to us," he lamented. "We had all the answers."

VOCALIST BILLY MILANO DOES NOT ATTEMPT TO SING FOR ONE SECOND. HE JUST YELLS LIKE TONY SOPRANO, AND THE LYRICS TO THE TITLE TRACK ARE FULLY OUT OF COMPLIANCE WITH MODERN-DAY WOKENESS REQUIREMENTS.

REVIEW

ANTHRAX

Spreading the Disease

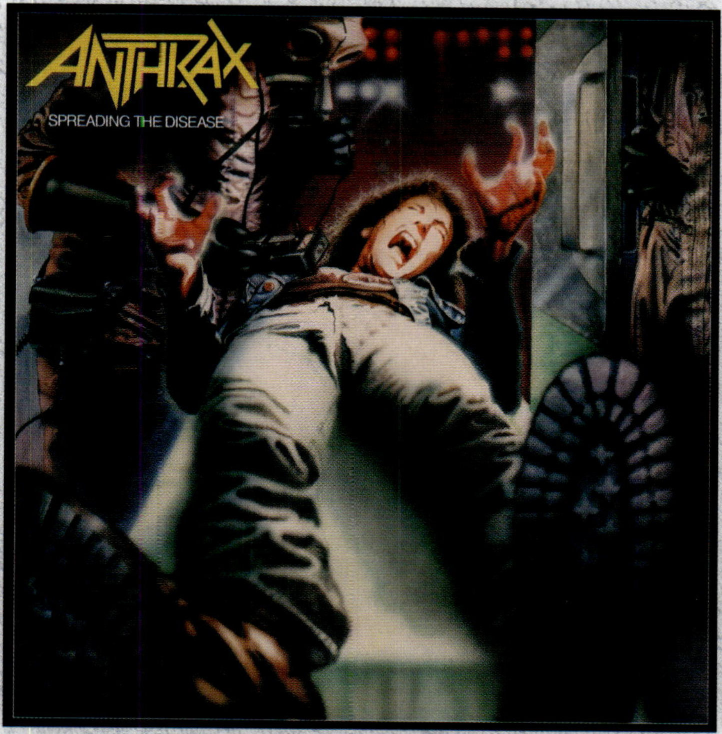

ANTHRAX'S SECOND STUDIO album was released on October 30, 1985, through Megaforce Records, and was their first record with vocalist Joey Belladonna and bassist Frank Bello. It shows the Anthrax sound in more refined form, so much so that if you listen to it immediately after *Fistful of Metal*, you might say, "Aaaaaah, this is more like it."

The record opens with "A.I.R.," which features strong melodic ideas from Belladonna, who cannot shake his Steve Perry-isms. Bello executes lots of fills and turnarounds in "Lone Justice" that are straight off *The Number of the Beast*, and he should be commended for using a different approach from that of his predecessor, who was a bludgeoner. That's not an insult to either one of them, by the way.

"Madhouse" is the song they made a music video for. It depicts the band playing in a facility resembling the set of *One Flew Over the Cuckoo's Nest*, with anxious patients wandering around to boot. Ian told *Metal Hammer* in 2024 that MTV refused to air it on the grounds that it made fun of the mentally ill. He said the band wasn't mad about the setback, nor was the label. Not only did it give them free publicity, but being banned was a badge of honor.

"We were very excited about it," he said. "I think the label put out a press release saying we were officially banned from MTV."

"S.S.C. / Stand or Fall" opens with an exotic guitar interlude by Dan Spitz, before becoming a strangely major-key exercise with upbeat choruses. It almost stands a chance of being called accessible. "Aftershock" is heavy and fast right from the jump, with lots of double bass. The thing that makes the record is the sound of Benante-Ian-Bello playing chugging rhythms, which could almost justify an entire record of its own.

Belladonna's performance on "Medusa" occasionally recalls Mike Reno from Loverboy, informing us that we've gotta do it his way or no way at all. The record ends with "Gung-Ho," the most hyped-up thrash song on the whole thing.

Overall, a more identifiable Anthrax sound is present here. There were no inept or incompetent musicians in the prior Anthrax incarnation, but the sound just didn't gel. This sounds like a band playing together, all at the same time, in the same room, and you can hear everything in equal balance. Joe Daly invoked not one but two different "M" words when describing it in *Metal Hammer* in 2024: "*Spreading The Disease* is a fist-pumping thrash masterpiece, combining infectious hooks with bold, intricate musicianship," he wrote.

MTV REFUSED TO AIR "MADHOUSE" ON THE GROUNDS THAT IT MADE FUN OF THE MENTALLY ILL. IAN SAID THE BAND WASN'T MAD, NOR WAS THE LABEL. NOT ONLY DID IT GIVE THEM FREE PUBLICITY, BUT BEING BANNED WAS A BADGE OF HONOR.

Kirk Hammett, Lars Ulrich, the new guy Jason Newsted, and James Hetfield keep their game faces.

CHAPTER 6

1986:

WE'LL SEE YOU TOMORROW IN DENMARK

Ozzy Osbourne, the Prince of Fucking Darkness, in his *Ultimate Sin*–era regalia of 1986. Laugh all you want, he still gave Metallica—and thrash itself—the keys to the kingdom when he had them open for his *Ultimate Sin* tour.

When 1986 began, it was Metallica's year. Their third album, *Master of Puppets*, had reached the US Top 40 albums chart, and though it's been said before, it bears repeating: that was with no radio airplay or MTV exposure, just fans buying the record because they loved the band.

They embarked on the *Damage, Inc.* tour, and on the first leg, they got an assist from heavy metal royalty. Ozzy Osbourne was on tour to support his album, *The Ultimate Sin*, and asked them to open. He told *Metal Hammer* in 2022 that it was clear Metallica would be big—all he had to see was the audience. "You could tell just from how the crowd reacted every night," the late Prince of Fucking Darkness said. "They're a great band."

Being taken out on the road by Osbourne legitimized Metallica. If he had been the head of an organized crime family, one could say that by taking Metallica on tour, he had "made" them. They were untouchable.

Black Sabbath made the same gesture to Anthrax, but that deserves some clarification. Osbourne's old bandmate, guitarist Tony Iommi, was the one original member left in Sabbath, which had experienced a major downturn. Their current album, *Seventh Star*, was credited to "Black Sabbath Featuring Tony Iommi," a complicated and drama-laden moniker that didn't do much to sell tickets. According to the Black Sabbath Online fan site, Anthrax only got to play seven of their fifteen North American dates. The rest were canceled.

Anthrax's booking agency responded by scheduling a tour a few weeks later. On May 29, they played London's Hammersmith Palais, and Bernard Doe of *Metal Forces* was there to see it. "It was immediately evident that this was to be one of the great metal gigs," he wrote. "An 1,100-strong audience was turned into a frenzy of thrashing bodies as Anthrax delivered an equal helping of classics from both of their studio albums . . . the band hurled themselves around the stage like men possessed."

Dan Spitz of Anthrax on March 28, 1986, at some club in Brooklyn called L'Amour that they might have played at a few times.

A very sweaty Anthrax (*from left*: Frank Bello, Dan Spitz, Scott Ian, Joey Belladonna, and Charlie Benante) gets hydrated backstage at L'Amour on March 28, 1986.

He added that he had just learned a very exciting tidbit of news. Metallica was set to tour the UK and Europe in September, and as if that weren't enough, they were bringing Anthrax with them. "Be there," he said. "The future of metal lies here."

Spreading the Disease was selling, and there was no denying that having major label distribution had a lot to do with that. Right on schedule, they were accused of selling out, which made them more determined than ever to make their next record utterly uncompromising. Anthrax devised an organizing principle for writing the material, which could be summed in five words: "Let's make that even faster," Ian said.

Megadeth faced similar accusations. Their new record, *Peace Sells . . . But Who's Buying?* reached #76 on the *Billboard* chart—pretty impressive for a band whose primary promotional apparatus was fan word of mouth. Still, to some early diehard fans, their success was a crime, one they compounded by allowing the title track's bass line to be used for the introduction to *MTV News*.

It was great for exposure but worthless for selling out. Despite the accusation that the band had sold its soul to the dollar, Mustaine said the band never saw one penny for their trouble. "MTV cut the song about one note short of the point where it would have been legally obligated to pay a royalty fee," he said.

Megadeth went out on the road to promote the album, which the guitarist said he preferred to being at home. For one thing, he had no home—no one in Megadeth lived at a fixed address. Touring may have been a grind, but he felt it was simpler to live out of a suitcase, unattached. Besides, Mustaine still had a Metallica-size chip on his shoulder to keep him going when the hours on the road got long and lonely.

"It wasn't enough for Megadeth to do well," he said. "I wanted Metallica to fail."

Metallica was nowhere near failure, but they were considering a significant change. Well, three of them were. In London, on the last night of their UK tour with Anthrax, Ian said Burton, Hammett, and Hetfield told him they were planning to fire Ulrich. The specifics of the problem were never revealed. However, in 2015, Hammett told Albany radio station PYX 106 that the story was true. Ulrich, meanwhile, said he wasn't aware of it at the time, nor did he care in the present. "It was just not something that was ever on my radar," he said.

The final resting place of Cliff Burton, a brilliant musician taken from us much too soon.

The plan was intended to take effect once the European leg of the tour was over. That began in Sweden on September 24 in Lund, followed by Lillestrom the next night. Ian said that typically, the bands would hang out after the gig and unwind for a bit before driving to the next city, but the night of the 26th, after their performance in Stockholm, the bus driver wanted to leave earlier to avoid an approaching storm.

"We'll see you tomorrow in Denmark," Ian said to them. Anthrax finished their set and cleared out.

Shortly after, Mustaine said he got a phone call from a woman named Metal Maria, who had worked with Megaforce. She was in tears. Metallica's tour bus had crashed after the Stockholm gig, and Burton had been killed.

"I just stood there, clutching the phone, feeling like someone had punched me in the stomach," he said.

While en route to Copenhagen, the Metallica bus reportedly hit a patch of ice as the musicians slept. The driver lost control, and Burton was ejected from the bus and pinned beneath it.

When Anthrax arrived at their hotel in Copenhagen the morning of the 27th, Ian said he saw their tour manager, who had just spoken to the promoter. Hammett and Hetfield were okay, and Ulrich was at the hospital with minor injuries. But their bassist was killed.

In 1993, Hetfield told David Fricke of *Rolling Stone* about that night. "I saw him dead," Hetfield said. "I saw the bus lying right on him. I saw his legs sticking out."

Ian said it made kicking Ulrich out of the band a nonstarter because, as Hetfield told him after the accident, "we can't lose two guys." Metallica resolved to find a new bassist and carry on.

Burton was laid to rest on October 7, 1986. The exact same day, Slayer's Def Jam debut, *Reign in Blood*, was released. Thrash metal had said goodbye to one of its brightest lights the day it also produced its darkest offering.

Initially, *Reign in Blood* almost didn't get released. Columbia Records refused to distribute it because of the opening track, "Angel of Death." The song was about Nazi doctor Josef Mengele, who perpetrated horrible atrocities upon prisoners at Auschwitz concentration camp, and while it didn't glorify him or his actions, just describing what he did against a musical backdrop was enough to make Columbia refuse to handle the record.

In 2021, producer Rick Rubin told *Metal Hammer* that Geffen Records jumped into the breach to distribute it. The controversy won the record a lot of publicity, which helped sell it, but at the same time, some listeners interpreted the song to mean the band members were Nazi sympathizers.

Hanneman told *Decibel* in 2006 that this was simply not true. His father had fought in World War II and his tales from the front were fascinating to the guitarist. His father even had battlefield artifacts plucked off Nazis he had killed, and it made an impression on the guitarist, to say the least. That experience informed the lyrics to "Angel of Death," and the guitarist said it got them inadvertently pegged as white nationalists. "Next thing I know, we're neo-Nazis," he said.

RIGHT: It's 1986, and Slayer (*clockwise from bottom*: Kerry King, Dave Lombardo, Jeff Hanneman, and Tom Araya) have released the greatest thrash metal album of all time, *Reign in Blood*. OPPOSITE: Metallica (*from left*: Jason Newsted, James Hetfield, Lars Ulrich, and Kirk Hammett) loiter in someone's lobby in December 1986.

King said that the perception stuck for a while and was hard to shake. It was especially difficult in certain parts of the world. "We got the most flak for it in Germany," he said. "People get this thought in their heads—especially in Europe—and you'll never talk them out of it."

Reign in Blood is notable for its massive upgrade in sound quality. Slayer consciously drowned their Metal Blade records in reverb in an attempt to out-Venom Venom, but Rubin's first decision in the studio was to turn that knob to zero. Suddenly, you could hear everything, and it was a revelation.

Rubin made another valuable contribution by insisting that the band play as fast as possible. The suggestion faced no opposition whatsoever. Music journalist Don Kaye told *Metal Hammer* why he thought the band was all for it. "I think their goal was to out-heavy and out-speed Metallica," he said.

The resulting ten-song record clocked in at less than twenty-nine minutes—so short that when it was released on cassette, it wasn't split up into side one and side two. They just put all ten songs on one side of the tape, then repeated them on the other side.

Reign in Blood entered the *Billboard* chart upon release. It didn't chart as high as *Master of Puppets* or *Peace Sells . . .* , but the fact that it was embraced by consumers at all was surprising to see. After all, it almost wasn't released due to its content. The truth is, it sold itself—all anyone had to do was hear it.

Drummer Paul Bostaph remembered hearing it for the first time on a boombox at a house party. He was immediately drawn to it, saying it sounded like nothing before it. Slayer had changed the rules, and he said that had implications for every aspiring thrash musician who wanted to make a mark.

"I stood in front of that box for the entire twenty-some-odd minutes," he recalled. "I [said], "We're fucked."

ABOVE: Dave Mustaine wakes up dead at the Fort Homer W. Hesterly Armory in scenic Tampa, Florida. The venue once hosted Andy Griffith and the Doors. LEFT: The original Megadeth lineup (*from left*: Chris Poland, Dave Mustaine, Gar Samuelson, and David Ellefson) tries to act normal for long enough to get a usable photo for Capitol Records' promotional apparatus. OPPOSITE: Megadeth (*from left*: Chris Poland, Dave Mustaine, and David Ellefson) in November 1986 at L'Amour in Brooklyn. Drummer Gar Samuelson would be easier to see if he hadn't just gotten his cymbals back from the pawn shop.

Slayer went on tour with New Jersey's Overkill to support the album. Their singer, Bobby "Blitz" Ellsworth, described the Slayer audience as "tough," the understatement of a lifetime. He said the reaction to Slayer didn't escalate. You were just suddenly thrown in at the deep end the second they started. "It was as if someone just pushed a button," he said.

While things seemed to be going according to plan, Lombardo made a surprise announcement. He was quitting the band.

He told *Metal Forces* in 1991 that he had gotten married earlier that year and then left for tour a few months later. The musician's lifestyle contrasted too sharply with domestic life for his comfort, and he gave his notice, forcing Slayer to hire Tony Scaglione of New Jersey's Whiplash to finish the tour.

Slagel told *Metal Hammer* in 2024 that there was no feeling of a big, happy family within Slayer to keep Lombardo personally engaged. If the four of them had been close friends, it might have been different, but the simple fact is they weren't. "The four guys didn't really hang around a lot with each other offstage; they weren't super-friendly," he said. "But clearly it worked. Once they got onstage or in the studio, it was magical."

Lombardo said that after quitting, an opportunity to join Megadeth presented itself, which would have made him the second member of Slayer to appear in that band. He might have been interested, but he said that when he watched them perform, he was put off by what he saw. "They looked in bad shape," he said. "They were all involved really badly in drugs."

At the end of October, Metallica wrapped up their auditions, choosing bassist Jason Newsted of Arizona thrash band Flotsam and Jetsam. He was a Metallica fan and greatly respected Burton's legacy, and his first appearance with the band was on November 8. Barely six weeks had passed since the bus accident.

Ian recalled talking to Hammett by phone shortly thereafter. Metallica was going back to make up the European dates they had missed, and they wanted Anthrax to take their rightful place alongside them. They said yes, and Ian saw Metallica take the stage to pick up where they had left off.

"They were absolutely triumphant," Ian said. "It felt like snatching victory out of the jaws of defeat."

ABOVE: James Hetfield and his ESP Explorer "EET FUK" guitar bring the chug to Phoenix, Arizona, while Jason Newsted (*background*) brings the throb. OPPOSITE: Jason Newsted, live and loud in Phoenix, Arizona—otherwise known as the home of his former band, Flotsam and Jetsam.

Megadeth (*from left*: Chris Poland, Dave Mustaine, and David Ellefson) at L'Amour in 1986. Aspiring guitarists, take comfort in the fact that even Mustaine has to look at the dots sometimes.

REVIEW

METALLICA

Master of Puppets

METALLICA'S THIRD ALBUM was released through Elektra Records on March 3, 1986. Radio and MTV wouldn't play it, but it reached #29 on the US *Billboard* chart all the same.

"Battery" opens side one with an acoustic guitar, and once the whole band kicks in, it sounds magnificent. Everything in the mix is right where it should be. The middle breakdown section is exceptional and the final section sees the band playing two alternating chords against a thrash beat that's absolutely damaging to hear.

The title track is about drug addiction, and if you've ever had the privilege of being around cokeheads, it's accurate. After about three and a half minutes of midtempo riffing, a slow, quiet, intricate section and expertly structured guitar solo establish themselves, and it's about the last thing you expect to hear. After developing for a bit, it gets *much* heavier, with a slow, down-picked guitar buildup that leads back to the fast stuff.

"Welcome Home (Sanitarium)" rounds out side one and it's one of the best songs on the record. It depicts someone locked up in a (wait for it) sanitarium, and it really takes you there. Hammett's guitar solos weep and you can feel the misery and isolation of the song's main character.

The tragically underrated "Disposable Heroes" starts side two. The lyrics are about a soldier fighting in a war, and while they don't reach the heights of "War Pigs," they're spiritually similar and just as timeless. The middle section, marked by Hetfield asking, "Why am I dying?" features excellent interplay among the musicians.

The best part happens after the song appears to end. After the final chorus comes an exceptionally fast section in which Ulrich makes unexpected, creative choices that ratchet up the tension along with the modulations in key. The song seems to end but then comes back even faster—you weren't expecting it to do that. Not one bit.

"Orion" is the showstopper. The main riff instantly hooks you, and about four minutes in, the crunching guitars give way to silence. Burton eases into an elegant bass figure overlaid with bending, harmonized guitars, and it's the most unexpected thing on the record. The command of dynamics, counterpoint, and harmony is both exquisite and shocking, and nothing like it ever happened again in thrash metal.

Master of Puppets is a uniformly original album for any genre. It transcends thrash without abandoning it, and it sets a bar for other thrash bands. None of them met it. "'Tallica's final album before the death of Cliff Burton was a game-changer," Nick Ruskell wrote in *Kerrang!* in 2020. "From here on, everything would be different."

THE TITLE TRACK IS ABOUT DRUG ADDICTION, AND IF YOU'VE EVER HAD THE PRIVILEGE OF BEING AROUND COKEHEADS, IT'S ACCURATE.

REVIEW

MEGADETH

Peace Sells . . . But Who's Buying?

LISTENERS WHO WORRIED that Dave Mustaine might mellow out after *Killing Is My Business . . . and Business Is Good!* were relieved to learn he was still as crabby as ever on Megadeth's second album, *Peace Sells . . . But Who's Buying?* and had a lot to get off his chest.

Released on September 19, 1986, it opens with "Wake Up Dead." Mustaine recites a tale of relationship woe, something the Other Big Three never did. It's also more composed and intricate, and one wonders whether he wasn't trying to leapfrog *Ride the Lightning* in that department. The song concludes with a stomping midtempo riff, and it's fantastic.

"The Conjuring" takes its time developing its way to the fast stuff. When that kicks in, it's hard not to get caught up in it, and the unusual dynamic transitions between sections do a lot to keep you on your toes. "Peace Sells" features Mustaine listing his transgressions against polite society, which are many. The thing is almost commercial by Megadeth 1986 standards.

"Devil's Island" recalls Candlemass before some up-tempo galloping; by this point, the listener is accustomed to the songs changing up every thirty seconds. Also, the guitar solos just keep coming. "Good Mourning / Black Friday" has a lovely, spacious opening that you know will only hang out for a hot minute, so don't get too comfortable. When it gets fast, the rhythm guitars harmonize weirdly under . . . a guitar solo!

The structure keeps shifting and changing, almost to the point where one wonders whether the arrangements on Metallica's *. . . And Justice for All* were as insanely complex as they were in an attempt to reverse-leapfrog Mustaine for his insolent insistence on trying to top *Ride the Lightning*, assuming that's what he was trying to do.

"Bad Omen" is a great showcase for Samuelson, who sadly never drummed on another Megadeth record. His playing is exotic and interesting, as is the guitar playing of Chris Poland, who would also leave after this record. Both use unusual touches that separate them from the pack, and it's unfortunate that the lineup fractured after this. Those two clearly had a lot to offer.

"I Ain't Superstitious," the Howlin' Wolf chestnut, proves conclusively that Megadeth should never cover anyone else's songs. The album ends with "My Last Words," which is the best song on the record. Ellefson really distinguishes himself here. He was never as out-there a bassist as Cliff Burton, but he always made his presence known, especially here.

"*Peace Sells . . .* is where thrash's angriest man truly laid down the gauntlet," Nick Ruskell wrote in *Kerrang!* in 2020. "Songs like 'Wake Up Dead' and the venomous, sarcastic 'Peace Sells' are thrash at both its most state-of-the-art and its snottiest."

REVIEW

SLAYER

Reign in Blood

REIGN IN BLOOD was released on October 7, 1986, through Def Jam Records. It starts with "Angel of Death," and Lombardo's double bass is a marvel throughout. The middle features a midtempo riff section with two full verses describing Josef Mengele's atrocities at a midtempo pace. When Araya says, "sickening ways to achieve the Holocaust," he does so with mustache-twirling relish.

That section stops abruptly, and suddenly everything is at a billion miles an hour as Hanneman and King trade solos back and forth. The lyrics indicate who plays which solo; this is a good thing because it's impossible to tell by listening to the song unless you know which speaker is doling out which chaotic, nonmusical lead. Also, the whammy bar at the end of the final solo sounds like a Mengele victim screaming, "No! No! Please stop!" to harrowing effect.

"Necrophobic" defies you to engage in the simple act of keeping up with it. The lyrics, like "strangulation, mutilation, cancer of the brain," come at you faster than you can read them off the lyric sheet, and the riff under it sounds more like a natural disaster than a musical instrument.

"Jesus Saves" is anchored by a riff that's no more than three notes and a turnaround, but those turnarounds make the song. The second guitar solo starts with a blues bend, which is jarring in its normalcy. That wraps side one, but if you owned the cassette, it transitioned directly into "Criminally Insane," whose ominous riffing in the middle section is beyond sick. In "Postmortem," Araya asks the listener, "Do you wanna die?" over wind-tunnel guitars, and it ends with a thunderclap that announces the arrival of "Raining Blood."

The song kicks in with double bass pounding your head in at what seems to be a pretty fast clip. Suddenly, the band seems to say, "fuck this," and does eight cymbal chokes to transition into a much higher tempo. The effect is both startling and hilariously funny. Most of the transitions and changeups on *Reign in Blood* can be described that way—they're so sudden and go so sideways that they're almost like slapstick gags.

After a stomping midtempo march, Araya says, "raining blood from a lacerated sky," and at that point it goes into an ending that's the fastest thing on the record. It was the fastest thing on most records. The guitars sound like gale-force winds and we're in territory that's almost not music anymore—it's the end of the world.

Buildings crumble, airplanes fall from the sky, and missiles launch themselves. It ends with a jump scare–worthy thunderclap and the sound of rain. If you owned the vinyl, the rain sound in the runout groove wouldn't stop until you took the record off.

Upon its release, Bernard Doe of *Metal Forces* called it "the most superior thrash product ever to hit vinyl." Decades later, the critics may have changed, but the sentiment remained the same. Nick Ruskell made a literary analogy in *Kerrang!* in 2020 that was right on the money: "'If you want a picture of the future,' wrote George Orwell in his book *1984*, 'imagine a boot stomping on a human face, forever,'" Ruskell wrote. "If you want to know what that would sound like, here it is in twenty-nine minutes and ten tracks of the most aggressive, middle-fingered, and thrilling music ever written."

Reign in Blood saw Slayer take thrash metal to its logical conclusion. While the genre didn't end with its release, it seemed impossible that anyone could top it. Of course, they inspired countless death-metal bands, all of whom set out to be faster and heavier than *Reign in Blood*, and all of them succeeded. But when you listened to this record in 1986 and heard the way it ended, it felt like the last word on thrash metal had been said, and Slayer said it.

THE GUITARS SOUND LIKE GALE-FORCE WINDS
AND WE'RE IN TERRITORY THAT'S ALMOST NOT MUSIC ANYMORE—
IT'S THE END OF THE WORLD.

Dave Mustaine brings Megadeth's *Peace Sells* tour to the University of Illinois–Chicago on February 12, 1987.

CHAPTER 7

1987: THE NEEDLE AND THE SPOON

1981 | 1982 | 1983 | 1984 | 1985 | 1986

In 1987, an ascendant Megadeth opened for Alice Cooper on his *Constrictor* tour. Cooper's alcohol-fueled 1970s shenanigans were the stuff of legend—at one point, he drank a bottle of whiskey a day and even landed in a mental institution. Luckily, when he finally got sober, it stuck.

He warned Mustaine and Ellefson that they were on a similar trajectory and that they might not survive it, as he did. "You can't keep up this pace," he said. "You're going to burn out or die."

Mustaine and Ellefson thanked him for the advice, then went right back to using. The guitarist said it was par for the course: "When you're an addict, you don't listen to people."

While Cooper could sniff out the telltale signs of young rockers in trouble, he may not have appreciated the depth of Megadeth's issues. Mustaine described one instance of ingesting heroin and then throwing up, a charming side effect of the drug. Rather than use the toilet, he did the deed in the nearby closet. He said that Poland then shoved him aside to begin a frenzied search through the bandleader's vomit with his bare hands. He had hidden away his heroin in the part of the closet Mustaine had spoiled and was hoping to rescue it.

This lineup did not survive the tour, and the band parted ways with Chris Poland and Gar Samuelson due to what Mustaine called "consequences of their drug use," claiming that Samuelson, who passed away in 1999, would pawn pieces of his drum kit to support his habit. The drummer never made a public statement to confirm or deny it, so we can never know his perspective. However, in a 2022 interview with *Classic Rock*, Mustaine said the allegation was true of both the drummer and Poland.

"Gar and Chris were selling [the musical equipment] for heroin," he said. "We had to go to all the neighborhood pawn shops to get that stuff back."

Samuelson's drum tech, Chuck Behler, knew the band's set and was able to hop into the fray at a moment's notice, so he became Megadeth's new skin-pounder overnight. After some false starts, they retained the services of a guitar teacher named Jeff Young, and the newly retooled band began putting together their next album.

They also appeared in the documentary *The Decline of Western Civilization Part II: The Metal Years*, which was released the following year. Directed by Penelope Spheeris, it's essential viewing, and appearing in it gave Megadeth a level of exposure they'd never had before. The movie poster even consisted entirely of a photo of Mustaine. In his memoir, he broke with tradition to say something nice, calling her a "genius." "She perfectly captured the feeling of that era, in all its glorious, self-destructive decadence," he said.

Slayer was also dealing with lineup issues of its own. Lombardo had vacated the drum throne, cut his hair, and started living the 9-to-5 life, and while the band had drafted another drummer to finish the tour, it just wasn't the same. In 1991, Lombardo told Borivoj Krgin of *Metal Forces* that Rubin was relentless in his attempts to win him back. Lombardo was essential to the band's sound and the producer was willing to offer him anything if he returned. Eventually, it was Lombardo's wife, Theresa, who convinced him to return. After one phone call to Rubin, he was back and the producer personally drove him to the rehearsal studio.

RIGHT: Slayer's Jeff Hanneman and Kerry King in Amsterdam on March 5, 1987. Drummer Dave Lombardo was briefly out of the band at this time, and *Reign in Blood* producer Rick Rubin moved mountains to get him back. **OPPOSITE:** Megadeth (*from left*: David Ellefson, Chris Poland, Gar Samuelson, and Dave Mustaine) backstage at Detroit's Joe Louis Arena on February 13, 1987.

LEFT: Megadeth's Chris Poland and Dave Mustaine onstage in Chicago during a moment of harmony during the *Peace Sells* tour. Sadly, it wouldn't last. BELOW: Dave Mustaine and David Ellefson onstage in 1987, prior to firing two bandmates for committing drug-related infractions similar to offenses they themselves had committed.

Metallica (*from left*: James Hetfield, Kirk Hammett, Jason Newsted, and Lars Ulrich) at the Monsters of Rock festival on August 22, 1987.

"It was like I never left," Lombardo said.

The statement was more of a double-edged sword than it appears. The band members were famously cool to one another personally, and it was still like that when the drummer came back, so yeah, it was like he never left. At the same time, no close relationships had been damaged, because there weren't any in Slayer to begin with.

"I tried every now and then to hang out with all the guys, but . . . it wasn't my thing," he said.

Lombardo clarified that it wasn't a three-against-one dynamic with him as the odd man out. Nobody in Slayer was close; the dynamic was that of coworkers. Musically, they were as unyielding as dried concrete and ten times as heavy. But personally? Eh.

Photographer Glen E. Friedman saw that dynamic up close when he did a publicity shoot with the band. He told *Decibel* in 2006 that while Lombardo's world-class drumming was essential, it was plain to see there was no interpersonal relationship to speak of. "I remember they didn't really like Dave that much at that time, but they also never denied that he was the perfect drummer for them," he said. "I guess they just didn't get along."

Jason Newsted was on the receiving end of a much more fraught dynamic. Metallica was a whirlwind of activity at this point, an already demanding situation now compounded by his new bandmates' unprocessed grief. Burton's death was a fresh, oozing wound, and Newsted described the band to *Metal Hammer* as "grief-stricken" and just trying to survive the audition process.

At his first gig, he received the warmest welcome imaginable from Ray and Jan Burton, his predecessor's parents. Jan approached him and gave him her blessing, saying, "We love you. . . . Please be safe."

Metallica's Jason Newsted onstage at Monsters of Rock at Castle Donington in 1987. He seems happy.

James Hetfield, Lars Ulrich, and Kirk Hammett soldier on in 1987, less than a year after the death of bassist Cliff Burton.

It was a good note to start on, but it was drowned out by the chaos. The band embarked for Japan, then spent the first six weeks of 1987 in Europe, finally finishing the *Damage, Inc.* tour in Gothenburg, Sweden. During that time, Newsted was subjected to cruel hazing at the hands of his new bandmates. In 2022, former Metallica tour manager John Schneider told *Classic Rock* that he had witnessed it all firsthand, and it had been brutal. "The razzing of Jason was terrible," he said. "They never really gave him a chance."

In 1989, Newsted told *Rolling Stone* that the hazing was finished, a relic of the band's 1986 tour of Japan. Maybe he hoped the "Newkid" status would end if he pronounced it dead in print. "It was a test all the time—windups from everyone to see if I could cut it," he said. "Everybody would go down to the bar to have sushi and sake for days and charge it to my room. We'd go to take pictures at the temples, and they'd all get in one taxi and make me ride by myself. This went on for a year. If I was going to buckle, they had to know. I took it, and that was that."

THE WORLDS STATE OF THE ART SPEED METAL BAND
MEGADETH
NOV. 28
+SANCTUARY
PORTLAND
8PM ALL AGES
PINE STREET THEATRE
TICKETS AT: GI JOES, GALLERIA JEAN MACHINE, 2ND AVE. RECORDS, MUSIC MILLENNIUM, ROCKPORT, AUDIO ADDICT (CORVALLIS), HOUSE OF RECORDS (EUGENE)
NOV. 29
+SANCTUARY
TACOM
8PM ALL AGES
TACOMA DOME Convention Cent
TICKETS AT: TICKETMASTER, FALLOUT, CELLOPHANE SQUARE, TIME TRAVELERS

ABOVE: ***From left*****: David Ellefson, Gar Samuelson, Chris Poland, and Dave Mustaine under the influence of no hard drugs whatsoever. OPPOSITE: Dave Mustaine in 1987, doing one half of the "pat your head while you rub your belly" trick.**

Hetfield told MTV in 2014 that, unfortunately, this initial dynamic never really changed in Newsted's entire fifteen-year tenure. "Right from the beginning, there was a lot of hazing that just separated him, and he was always thought of as 'the new guy,'" he said.

Hammett said it was all a product of misdirected grief, which caused a spike in the band's already considerable alcohol intake. "There was so much anger because of Cliff's death," Hammett told *Louder* in 2022. "That kicked the drinking up two or three notches. Between 1987 and 1990, we were raging alcoholics."

Clearly, the surviving band members were in a terrible state. Why didn't they take some time off to regroup?

"We didn't understand the process of grieving or the process of pain," Ulrich told *Loud and Quiet*'s Daniel Dylan Wray in 2018. "We basically just kept going, put the blinders on, compartmentalized everything, and then just jumped in the nearest vodka bottle and off we went."

Too many commitments were already lined up anyway. Their profile had increased significantly and nobody wanted to lose the momentum. Burton's hard work and commitment had helped get Metallica to this point, and letting all that organic, DIY effort fall by the wayside was not an option. So all commitments made when Burton was alive were now being fulfilled, and the pace was unrelenting.

"By the time I got in, we were rolling," Newsted told the *Talk Toomey* podcast in 2021. "I was home for twenty days a year."

Anthrax (*clockwise from top*: Charlie Benante, Scott Ian, Dan Spitz, Frank Bello, and Joey Belladonna) clown around backstage at Chicago's Aragon Ballroom in December 1987 after the release of their breakthrough *Among the Living* album.

Ulrich also said that as much of a burden as it might have been to go right out on the road just weeks after Burton's passing, it was what they all wanted.

"You're twenty-three years old, full of spunk, ready to go, shit is happening, and being on the road is this free, autonomous place where you don't have to do anything other than play music and travel around," Ulrich told *Loud and Quiet*. "We were raring to go."

When the band came back, they intended to start work on their next studio album. Before they could make much progress, Hetfield sustained a broken arm while skateboarding. Ulrich noted it in a March 23, 1987, entry on his typewritten timeline of notable dates in Metallica history as "Second broken arm (James)."

They played the hand they were dealt and did the closest thing to taking a break that their DNA would allow, recording an EP of cover songs, released on August 21, 1987, under the name *The $5.98 E.P.: Garage Days Re-Revisited*. It peaked at #28 on the *Billboard* Top 200, one slot higher than *Master of Puppets*' 1986 peak. They hadn't lost a step.

On November 17, 1987, they released *Cliff 'Em All* on glorious VHS, which triumphantly slew Betamax in the bloody format wars of that storied decade. The video features the band in live performance with Burton, including the 1985 Day on the Green. It was a rare look backward from a band normally fixed on the future.

The members of Anthrax were affected by Burton's passing in their own way. The bus accident was fresh on their minds when they entered the studio in October 1986 to record *Among the Living*. "Cliff's death hit me hard," Scott Ian said.

The album featured the song "A.D.I./Horror of It All," likely the first song ever recorded about Burton's passing. Upon the record's release, it would be dedicated to their fallen comrade.

To helm the effort, the band enlisted Eddie Kramer, who had produced some of Ian's favorite Kiss albums. He loved the unobtrusiveness of his other work and wanted the same thing for Anthrax. "When you played a record he worked on, it sounded like the band was right there in your room," he said.

The band was well-rehearsed, so when they recorded, the performances were tight, energetic, and belligerent. When Kramer told them he had a rough mix to play back, they couldn't wait to hear it, but when he pressed play, the proceedings dripped with reverb, neutering the sound. The band knew this was *the* Eddie Kramer and telling him how a record should sound was like telling a Michelin three-star chef to put more ketchup on a steak. Still, they insisted that all the effects had to go.

Kramer obliged and the effect was the same as the one Slayer achieved when Rubin expelled all the reverb from *Reign in Blood*. It was a tight, precise sound that offered no separation between the listener and the music. No helmet, no seatbelt, no nothing. Just pain.

"It sounded fucking great," Ian said. The guitarist said the producer added minimal touches to enhance a couple of things, but otherwise it was a no-frills affair. It sounded like you were sitting in their rehearsal space.

The band also recorded the rap parody "I'm the Man" during those sessions. Ian and his guitar tech, John Rooney, were screwing around once at Ian's home and wrote rap lyrics about being in Anthrax. It just kind of came together. "I plugged in my guitar and played the Jewish folk song 'Hava Nagila' while John continued to rap," he recalled.

There was no intention of putting it on *Among the Living*. The band had considered offering it to the Beastie Boys, who were Slayer's Def Jam labelmates, but they ultimately kept it for themselves. It was eventually put on the B-side of the 12-inch single release of "I Am the Law," because, after all, it was just a novelty song, and that's why god invented B-sides.

Anthrax had inadvertently emulated Kiss. "Beth" was the throwaway B-side to "Detroit Rock City" that became a hit only when a DJ played the wrong side of the single by mistake, causing the radio station's phone lines to light up. Anthrax's throwaway B-side was not a syrupy ballad but a smartass tribute to rap music, and it improved their fortunes as well. At that year's Monsters of Rock festival, they saw that the crowd of 80,000 not only loved it but knew every word. "To this day it's probably our most requested song," Ian said in 2015.

The song was a lot of fun, something that set Anthrax apart from the other Big Four bands. When Anthrax performed "I'm the Man," they really seemed to enjoy themselves. Ian once observed that "there's no smiling in Slayer," but in the Big Four, Anthrax had cornered the market on fun, laughter, and merriment.

The song was also one of the first-ever recorded examples of rap-metal. Run-DMC had sampled Aerosmith's "Walk This Way" in 1986, an early fusion of rap and hard rock, but it seemed like a one-off and didn't suggest a new genre was in the making. "I'm the Man" did.

Anthrax toured in 1987 with Exodus and Celtic Frost. In contrast to the small clubs where they started out, they were now playing venues like the Springfield Civic Center in Massachusetts, which had a capacity of 10,000. Mainstream acceptance was on the horizon.

While Anthrax didn't get a chance to work with the Beastie Boys on "I'm the Man," there was nonetheless overlap between the Beasties and a Big Four group. King played on *Licensed to Ill*, contributing lead guitar to "Fight for Your Right" and "No Sleep till Brooklyn." "[Rubin] paid me a couple hundred bucks to come into the studio," King told *Decibel* in 2006. "That was a lot of money to me."

Anthrax (*from left*: Frank Bello, Joey Belladonna, Charlie Benante, Dan Spitz, and Scott Ian) in 1987, riding the high of a well-received album and the popularity of "I'm the Man."

King appears briefly in the "No Sleep till Brooklyn" music video, which went into heavy rotation immediately. It was likely the first time anyone from MTV Nation ever saw a member of Slayer, in any capacity.

The partnership with Rubin had resulted in some great opportunities, even if the band didn't like them. One was covering Iron Butterfly's "In-A-Gadda-Da-Vida" for the *Less Than Zero* soundtrack. "Kerry fucking hates it," Hanneman said.

King confirmed his fellow guitarist's assessment: He fucking hated it.

"There are a lot better things to judge us by than that hunk of shit," he groused.

Be that as it may, King acknowledged that from a business perspective, it was the right move. It got Slayer radio play, which came in handy when their next record came out. Besides, as much as King hated the Iron Butterfly cover, Hanneman hated their 2002 recording of Steppenwolf's "Born to Be Wild" even more. "I can't believe we did that," he said.

Despite the concessions, Slayer was not accepted by the mainstream in 1987 or any other time. Anthrax, Megadeth, and Metallica all made inroads, thanks to their use of melody, but Slayer never did. It would be more accurate to say that the mainstream grudgingly recognized Anthrax, Megadeth, and Metallica's right to exist, which afforded Slayer the opportunity to sneak in behind them. As the not entirely accurate saying goes, a rising tide lifts all boats.

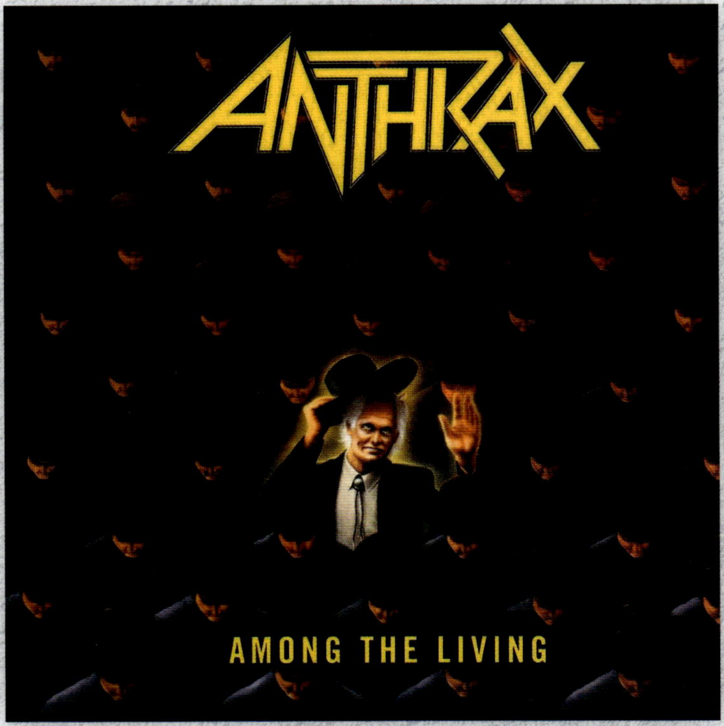

REVIEW

ANTHRAX

Among the Living

AMONG THE LIVING is a joyfully anarchic record that couples the high-speed thrash of *Speak English or Die* with an actual singer, verses, and choruses. The production is clear throughout, the drums are jarringly in your face, and there is chugging, down-picked guitar as far as the eye can see.

The speedy stuff is taken at a D.R.I. tempo (translation: very fast). You feel like you're just barely keeping up with it, and will never overtake it. "Indians" is excellent from its melodic opening to its brick-heavy riffing, and the same goes for "Caught in a Mosh" and "Imitation of Life." Even songs like "I Am the Law" and "A Skeleton in the Closet," which have periodic lulls during the midtempo verses, are utterly redeemed by the fast bits, which abruptly abduct you out of nowhere before you even know what hit you.

There are issues. "One World" is dull, and the NYHC-inspired lyrics have aged poorly, although not for the same reasons as the intentionally offensive ones on *Speak English or Die*. They're contrived, which is worse. The lyric "Instead of thinking S.D.I., he should be thinking of peace" is as Reagan-era and musically clumsy as it gets, and while many Gen Xers fondly recall hardcore music's exhortations against the Gipper, they mean nothing today.

The other problem is lead guitarist Dan Spitz. He's plenty adept and fleet-fingered, but every time he steps up, it sounds like he's rehearsing scales, none of which have any relation to the songs in which they appear. In fact, bassist Frank Bello said that the name of the introduction to "A.D.I./Horror of It All" was inspired one day when Spitz was preoccupied with playing Arabian scales. "I just said, that's 'Arabian Douche Intro,'" he told KSDT radio in 1988.

Among the Living was Anthrax's breakthrough, and deservedly so. It put them on equal footing with Megadeth, Metallica, and Slayer, all of whom released breakthrough albums in 1986. For that reason, this 1987 album is spiritually part of the class of 1986, just as *Speak English or Die* is spiritually a Big Four album. While you may disagree, no one could argue with the assessment of the record that drummer Charlie Benante gave the *Aquarian* in 2015. "That was the record that gave us a career," he said.

AMONG THE LIVING PUT ANTHRAX ON EQUAL FOOTING WITH MEGADETH, METALLICA, AND SLAYER, ALL OF WHOM RELEASED BREAKTHROUGH ALBUMS IN 1986.

REVIEW

METALLICA

The $5.98 E.P.: Garage Days Re-Revisited

METALLICA'S FIRST RELEASE to feature Jason Newsted was an intentionally low-maintenance, covers-only effort.

It kicks off with Diamond Head's "Helpless," which barrels along with destructive glee and easily defies its six-and-a-half-minute running time. The slow, lumbering Holocaust song "The Small Hours" is up next, and despite its ominous crunch, it has melodic elements that new listeners could latch onto. That's all that's on side one, but you don't feel shortchanged by the brevity, because it's perfect. In fact, if FM radio DJs still played "perfect album sides," this would be eligible.

Side two doesn't fare as well. The cover of Killing Joke's "The Wait" kind of drags, and Budgie's "Crash Course in Brain Surgery" is compromised by its middle section. In the original, Burke Shelley sings some boilerplate "yeah baby" stuff in a chipmunk squeal that makes Geddy Lee sound like Barry White. Hetfield doesn't sing any of that, so the breakdown section consists entirely of context-free pauses that don't make sense. On the plus side, it starts with loud, authoritative bass from Newsted, which, as we shall see in the following chapters, marked the last time anyone would hear him on a Metallica record for the next four years.

The EP ends with "Last Caress / Green Hell," a joyously chaotic medley of Misfits songs that's engaging right from the opening line about having something to say. If people still made Metallica mixtapes, they would do well to end them all with this song.

Despite a couple of lulls, *The $5.98 E.P.: Garage Days Re-Revisited* is the final, rollicking entry from Metallica before they broke wide open. Despite its status as a "not very produced" stopgap EP with no new original material, it remains an essential entry in the band's catalog.

"LAST CARESS / GREEN HELL" IS A JOYOUSLY CHAOTIC MEDLEY OF MISFITS SONGS THAT'S ENGAGING RIGHT FROM THE OPENING LINE ABOUT HAVING SOMETHING TO SAY.

Dave Mustaine engulfed in dry ice and playing a double-neck guitar in 1988, a year that would prove a tad tumultuous for Megadeth—1989 would be even worse!

CHAPTER 8

1988: GENUINELY OFFENSIVE SATANIC DRIVEL

1981 | 1982 | 1983 | 1984 | 1985 | 1986

On January 19, 1988, Megadeth released *So Far, So Good . . . So What!* featuring new drummer Chuck Behler and new guitarist Jeff Young. That same year, *The Decline of Western Civilization Part II: The Metal Years* featured Megadeth prominently alongside Alice Cooper, Ozzy Osbourne, Lemmy Kilmister, and Faster Pussycat. Fans of the other artists in the film learned of Megadeth's existence for the first time, and being immortalized in celluloid gave the band a permanence that no amount of live performances could.

If for no other reason than that, 1988 was a good year for Megadeth, but they had other positive developments to be grateful for as well. They had a well-received album, and while lineup overhauls aren't always accepted by fans, the Megadeth faithful didn't hold this one against them. They had survived a lineup shift and made a classic record, and they would be playing August dates on the *Monsters of Rock* tour.

Things were looking up. Had new blood ushered in an era of enduring stability for this beleaguered band at long last?

The short answer was "no." After what Dave Mustaine estimated was less than a year, the lineup disintegrated.

The problems began after their opening performance on the *Monsters of Rock* tour at Castle Donington. Ellefson announced he was leaving the tour to enter rehab, which, by extension, meant Megadeth would be leaving as well. "This was one of the biggest tours in the history of metal, and Megadeth had pulled its own plug," Mustaine said.

RIGHT: Joey Belladonna rocking his band's latest swag on December 3, 1988, as Anthrax open for Ozzy on the No Rest for the *Wicked* tour in New Haven, Connecticut. OPPOSITE: Megadeth's *So Far, So Good . . . So What!* lineup (*clockwise from top left*: Chuck Behler, Jeff Young, Dave Mustaine, and David Ellefson) was sadly short-lived. But they look so happy!

Metallica's James Hetfield serenades the Los Angeles Memorial Coliseum on July 24, 1988, during the *Monsters of Rock* tour.

The lineup fractured after that, due to what the guitarist called "personality conflicts fueled primarily by drugs and alcohol." Mustaine did not specify whose personality, drugs, or alcohol, but he did say that Young had made some sort of perverted phone call to his then-fiancée Diana, precipitating his ouster.

"[Young] told her that he fantasized about having sex with her while he was screwing his girlfriend," Mustaine said. "You don't shit where you eat, and you don't try to fuck your bandmate's fiancée. Especially when your bandmate is your boss."

In a 2009 interview with *Metal Underground*, Young addressed that and other allegations Mustaine had made about him. "He really tries to go out of his way to discredit people to cover his tracks," Young said. "I think that some of it is just malicious, and other times I don't think he remembers it right because he was so high."

As for Behler, Mustaine attributed his ouster to substance abuse. The drummer has remained unfailingly quiet about the sordid goings-on in the band and has never addressed any claims made against him. In a very rare comment that he made to *Brave Words* in 2009, he clarified that there will likely never be a tawdry tell-all memoir about the *So Far, So Good . . . So What!* lineup under his name. "I really don't think people are too interested in hearing about the petty little things that happened between us back then," he said.

While Megadeth geared up for the ultimately aborted tour, Slayer released *South of Heaven*. They had wisely concluded that trying to top *Reign in Blood* was a fool's errand, so the album took a big stylistic change in direction. In fact, the very first song was taken at a slow tempo.

Anthrax (*from left*: Joey Belladonna, Dan Spitz, and Scott Ian) at the Monsters of Rock festival in Tilburg, Netherlands, on September 4, 1988. Belladonna has Iroquois blood, so he gets a pass on the outdated nomenclature for Indigenous peoples of the Americas that you see on his hat.

That wasn't the only change. Araya's aggressive bark was still there, but on the slower stuff, he was singing. No one would mistake him for Ronnie James Dio, but he was dispensing discernible vocal melodies, and the approach worked without compromising the music's effect.

Slayer may have toned down a smidgen, but their live audiences didn't act like it. *New York Times* writer Jon Pareles was in attendance at an August 31, 1988, show at New York City's Felt Forum and noted that, toward the end of the show, dozens of square projectiles were being flung from the seating area at the back of the venue. "In the latter part of the show, cushions torn out of the seats in the stands started flying through the air," he said.

The incident became known to some as the "Cushion Riot," as author D.X. Ferris called it in his 2013 book, *Slayer 66 2/3: The Jeff & Dave Years*. A couple of weeks prior, there had been a riot outside the Hollywood Palladium that resulted in the group being banned from the venue until 2013, thanks in part to "brawls with the police going on outside," per the *Los Angeles Times*' Janiss Garza.

The "Cushion Riot" got more press at the time and even to this day perhaps in part because there's video of it on the official Slayer website. In fact, the entire show is available on YouTube. Furthermore, the author of this book was there and can attest to everything that was reported.

Slayer's Jeff Hanneman, live and in person, in 1988. He always insisted that the lyrics to "Angel of Death" were not intended to glorify Josef Mengele, but did anyone listen?

Joey Belladonna uses illustrative body language on December 3, 1988, during Anthrax's stint as openers for the late, great Ozzy Osbourne.

"It certainly didn't compare to the property damage and unrest that took place outside the Hollywood Palladium," Ferris wrote. "But it's easy to understand why they recall it as a riot."

It started when an unidentified fan somewhere in the back tore out one seat cushion and threw it. Countless light bulbs immediately illuminated over audience members' heads and moments later dozens of cushions took flight. The author compared the spectacle to "seagulls zooming over a beach," and not even Slayer could stop it. Araya tried talking some sense into the crowd, to no avail.

"Give us a break," he pleaded. "We can probably never play here again."

He was smacked by a seat cushion, mid-plea. Almost three decades later, in 2015, he told *The Quietus* that any type of pleading for decorum with Slayer fans is futile because they'll take it as encouragement. "All they'll hear is, 'Do it again,'" he said. "'DO IT MORE! He likes what we're doing!'"

As Araya announced the encore, "Angel of Death," the security lining the stage did their level best to act as human shields from the flying cushions. "Good night, assholes," Araya signed off.

Howie Abrams, former A&R representative for Warner Bros., was there and said there was a perceptible atmosphere of menace at the Felt Forum that night. "It seemed as if half the crowd was on angel dust and just didn't give a fuck about their own safety, much less anyone else's," he said. "I don't recall seeing as many bloodied, passed-out, and fucked-up kids in one building as I saw at this infamous show."

Slayer indeed never played the venue again, as Araya had predicted. However, despite losing the battle, they won the war. Anthrax, Megadeth, and Metallica all hosted riots or near-riots of their own at one time or another, but Slayer, who had already earned a reputation as the most extreme Big Four group, could also boast the most deranged fans.

Dan Spitz of Anthrax, live in Pamplona, Spain. Sadly, because this performance took place on September 17, 1988, the band was two months too late to see the running of the bulls.

While Metallica had been accused of selling out since their second album, the reality was that, in 1988, the mainstream was as afraid of them as they were of Slayer. Despite their Top 40 achievements, they were still perceived as an outlaw band. "The mainstream hadn't caught up to us yet, so we all still felt like outsiders," Ulrich told *Loud and Quiet*'s Daniel Dylan Wray in 2018.

That ended on September 7, 1988, with the release of *. . . And Justice for All*, which reached #6 on the *Billboard* 200, something unthinkable even a year earlier.

In no universe was it a radio-friendly album. All nine songs were complex epics, two of which spanned almost ten minutes. Then there was the mix. Completely dry and with no audible bass guitar, it was nothing but trebly drums that sounded like a typewriter and layer upon layer of scooped guitars. According to coproducer Flemming Rasmussen, all of that was on purpose, but it wasn't because Newsted's performance was subpar and had to be buried in the mix.

"I'm probably one of the only people in the world, including Jason and Toby Wright, the assistant engineer, who heard the bass tracks on *. . . And Justice for All*," he told *Metal Hammer* in 2016. "They are fucking brilliant."

Since then, much ink has been expended trying to explain the baffling decision. Were they hazing the new bassist? Were they so grief-stricken that they couldn't make good decisions? The explanation Hetfield gave to *Louder* in 2022 seems the most likely. "We mixed that record while we were on the road," he said. "That's not an excuse for the way that it sounds, but our ears were beat."

When Newsted heard the completed *. . . And Justice for All* for the first time, let's just say he was displeased. But there was no slowing down at that point. The runaway momentum left no time to remix and the record had to go out the door as it was, like it or not.

"We were firing on all cylinders," Newsted explained. "I was just rolling with it and going forward."

Jason Newsted of Metallica in 1988, performing in front of too many people to care if his bass was audible on the band's new record, . . . *And Justice for All* (it wasn't).

In 2022, Hammett conceded that he didn't like the mix, and the passage of more than three decades hadn't changed his mind. "The way it sounds is funky," he said. "Funky as in bad, not funky as in groovy."

Ultimately, it didn't matter. In 2013, Newsted told *Loudwire* that he had long since taken the 10,000-foot view on the affair. He said a fan gave him a copy of a widely circulated recording known alternately as . . . *And Justice for Jason* and . . . *And Jason for All*, which plops the album's isolated bass tracks from *Guitar Hero: Metallica* atop the officially released bass-free mix. On some versions, disgruntled fans took it upon themselves to just record their own bass over the album. Both versions thoroughly rehabilitate the record, giving it color and movement the released version sorely lacks.

Newsted said the fan told him the bootleg recording was "how it was supposed to be." The bassist appreciated the gesture but disagreed with the assessment. "I think how it was supposed to be is how it came out and how it made the mark on the world," he said. "But cool, bass in it? Thank you."

Anthrax found their 1988 album compromised by the demands of their schedule as well. It would prove to be a hectic year, pretty much from the moment it started, when Kiss's people called Anthrax's people to ask if they would open for them on the *Crazy Nights* tour. What had once seemed like an unattainable fantasy to Ian was now becoming a reality. His younger self would never have thought it possible that he might not just meet Kiss bassist Gene Simmons but share a stage with him. But now here he was, and he got to meet his idol in the catering area.

They talked about various topics, eventually getting around to their shared upbringing in the borough of Queens. He learned that Simmons's mother lived right next to Bayside High School, where an adolescent Dan Lilker learned the word "anthrax."

That April, after returning from the tour, they began work on their next record, planning to release it just ahead of their August

Metallica (*from left*: Jason Newsted, James Hetfield, Lars Ulrich, and Kirk Hammett) on September 17, 1988, in Pamplona, the Spanish city depicted in Ernest Hemingway's *The Sun Also Rises*. Every Metallica fan knows that, of course.

dates with Iron Maiden. Ian and Benante have both said it caused a rushed process and neither considers the album properly finished.

"If we had maybe two or three months more to spend on it, I think it would have been a great album," Benante told the *Aquarian* in 2015.

The record, *State of Euphoria*, was released on September 18, 1988, just after the release of . . . *And Justice for All*. It sold very well, but despite its success, Ian was in the strange position of feeling like the fans were wrong about the record they were snapping up excitedly. "Instead of following our creative instincts, we let the music business dictate what we were doing," he said.

While he may never be happy with the record that resulted, he said the Iron Maiden tour was a great tonic for it. "We were playing to sold-out stadiums of people losing their minds to Anthrax," he said. "We were selling hundreds of thousands of records and selling truckloads of merch. We had 'made it.'"

1981 | 1982 | 1983 | 1984 | 1985 | 1986

The crowd at Monsters of Rock at Castle Donington on August 20, 1988. Megadeth's participation in the tour that year started and ended that same night.

REVIEW

MEGADETH

So Far, So Good . . . So What!

IN 1988, MEGADETH faced the same question that Anthrax, Metallica, and Slayer faced after releasing breakthrough albums: What do we do for an encore? *Peace Sells . . . But Who's Buying?* had put them on the map—the follow-up had to keep them there.

So Far, So Good . . . So What! was released on January 19, 1988, and 75 percent of it still holds up. In fact, two absolutely essential tracks guarantee its lifetime membership in thrash metal Valhalla. The first is the proggy instrumental opener, "Into the Lungs of Hell." It's incredibly engaging, and even if it had been followed by seven absolutely godawful songs, which it wasn't, it would still be an indispensable classic.

The other towering achievement is "In My Darkest Hour." In 2017, Mustaine told *Rolling Stone* he was inspired to write it after learning of Cliff Burton's death from someone other than his former Metallica bandmates. He might have been fired from the band in the harshest and most traumatic way possible, but he was still hurt that neither James nor Lars had thought to call him personally to let him know what had happened.

"I took it very, very, very bad," he said. "The 'darkest hour' in the song is me knowing that I was alone."

There are, sadly, a couple of absolutely pungent stinkers on the record. One is the ill-advised cover of the Sex Pistols' "Anarchy in the U.K.," which sounds as studied and tight-assed as Howlin' Wolf being performed by the London Symphony Orchestra. The other is "Liar." A not so thinly veiled swipe at former guitarist Chris Poland, the lyrics list "hocking guitars" among several other accusations against him.

Poland told *The David Ellefson Show* in 2025 that the dis track had hamstrung him later in his career, recalling a long-ago incident in which he approached Carvin Guitars for an endorsement deal and was brutally rebuffed. "I spoke to the guy, and he goes, 'Dude, we don't use people like you on our roster,'" he said.

Poland concluded by saying that for all the problems that went down during his tenure in Megadeth, he had but one regret. "I regret that Mustaine, for years, would go on stage and call me a liar," he said.

TWO ABSOLUTELY ESSENTIAL TRACKS GUARANTEE THIS ALBUM'S LIFETIME MEMBERSHIP IN THRASH METAL VALHALLA: "INTO THE LUNGS OF HELL" AND "IN MY DARKEST HOUR."

REVIEW

SLAYER

South of Heaven

IN 1988, SLAYER had the unenviable task of following up *Reign in Blood*. *South of Heaven* deviated from the extreme speed and chaos of its predecessor, but don't worry—it still alienated plenty of people.

Slayer had decided that rather than try to outrun the 1986 record, they needed to do something different, so while "Silent Scream," "Live Undead," and "Ghosts of War" would fit alongside "Necrophobic," much of the rest of the record would not.

The opening and closing tracks, "South of Heaven" and "Spill the Blood," represent the biggest departures. They go for mood and atmosphere, and while they don't clear the bar set by Black Sabbath with their debut album's title track, it was still a sea change. Luckily, most of the fandom was cool with it.

Another major change came courtesy of vocalist Tom Araya. He had opened *Reign in Blood* with an eardrum-rupturing shriek, the kind that makes you call 911 if you hear it emanating from next door. His approach here was far removed from that. He was actually *singing* much of the time, and for hardcore fans, the sound of him carrying a tune was almost as shocking as the opening shriek on "Angel of Death" had been to everyone else. But most of the fandom was cool with that, too.

People who were not fans gave Slayer zero points for evolving. Kim Neely of *Rolling Stone* gave *South of Heaven* a review better suited to a Darkthrone album, calling the band "a depraved lot given to creepy ramblings about blood sacrifice and rotting flesh."

Before concluding that the new Guns N' Roses album was better, she said something meant to be dismissive of the band. Unfortunately for her, most Slayer fans likely considered it the equivalent of giving the record 666 stars out of 10: "[*South of Heaven* is] a cacophony of genuinely offensive satanic drivel," she wrote.

Victory!

TOM ARAYA HAD OPENED REIGN IN BLOOD WITH AN EARDRUM-RUPTURING SHRIEK, THE KIND THAT MAKES YOU CALL 911. HIS APPROACH HERE WAS FAR REMOVED FROM THAT.

"FOR ALL SAD WORDS
OF TONGUE OR PEN,
THE SADDEST ARE THESE,
'IT MIGHT HAVE BEEN.'"

—John Greenleaf Whittier, "Maud Muller," 1856

REVIEW

METALLICA

. . . And Justice For All

IN 1988, SLAYER'S Tom Araya and Kerry King were interviewed in England by Canada's SuperChannel. While fielding the interviewer's questions about everything Slayer, such as, "What is the criteria for your lyrics?" (King's answer: "To be disgusting. To be offensive."), she asked what they thought of Metallica, who had just released *. . . And Justice for All*.

"It's a little off the wall for me," Araya said. "It's just something I never expected."

Indeed, few people expected what they got with 1988's *. . . And Justice for All*. Bone-dry, completely lacking bass (both the instrument and the frequency), and bearing the second-worst drum sound in Metallica history, it sounds like a demo with guitar solos overdubbed. The mix sucks and undermines what could have been a masterpiece.

Nonetheless, there's some good stuff. The title track has all kinds of neat, mutating riffs that play with mixed meters and abruptly changing tempos, and Hetfield and Ulrich are 100 percent locked in with one another the entire time. In the places where they chug along in unison, such as on "Blackened" and "Eye of the Beholder," they sound like the heavy machinery that tore off Tony Iommi's fingertips.

. . . And Justice for All has two centerpieces. One is the penultimate song, "To Live Is to Die," which features the final fragments of Cliff Burton's songwriting. Like the title track, it defies its almost ten-minute running time and is a diverting listen throughout.

The other is "One." Its primary feature is the middle section, in which the guitars and Ulrich's kick drums operate in a uniform pattern that approximates machine-gun fire. Longtime thrash metal fans may have recognized that bit as a "tribute" (cough, cough) to the title track from Dark Angel's 1986 album *Darkness Descends*, but to those brand-new to thrash metal, it was like nothing ever. To this day, that part of the song still hooks people.

The production on *. . . And Justice for All* absolutely sucks and makes Black Sabbath's *Born Again* sound like it was produced by George Martin. No speaker system on earth can redeem it. If the absence of a remix in the thirtieth-anniversary box set is any indication, we will never get one.

Regardless, it broke through, was embraced by millions, and influenced countless bands. Take it or leave it.

REVIEW

ANTHRAX

State of Euphoria

STATE OF EUPHORIA was released on September 19, 1988, making it the last album released that year by a Big Four band. The performances and production are top-notch, so no problems there.

Unfortunately, the songs aren't there, although "Be All, End All" and "Antisocial" still pop up in live sets. In 2018, Charlie Benante told *Billboard* that the record fell short of the band's hopes and expectations. "All of us in the band felt that it was not finished," he said. "We could have used a little more time with it."

Ian calls the record "shitty" in his memoir. Having said that, Benante felt that too much had been made over the years about the band not being thrilled with the record. "We don't hate this record at all," Benante told *The Rockpit* in 2018. "There's some great moments on this album."

When it came out, critics weren't feeling it. Today, they still aren't. Steve Huey wrote on *AllMusic* that it was a disappointment, and the ways in which it was equal to its predecessor were not the good ways. "The lyrics continue the self-consciously intellectual, PC approach begun on *Among the Living*," he wrote.

Not everyone felt that way. Bernard Doe of *Metal Forces* thought it was outstanding and gave it 10 out of 10. "*State of Euphoria* is without a doubt Anthrax's finest work to date," he wrote. "The powerful 'Now It's Dark,' the excellent 'Schism,' with its onslaught of razor-sharp riffing, and the pounding of 'Misery Loves Company' all shine through with flying colors . . . the last song on the album, 'Finale,' is possibly Anthrax's best ever . . . a fitting climax to the year's best release so far."

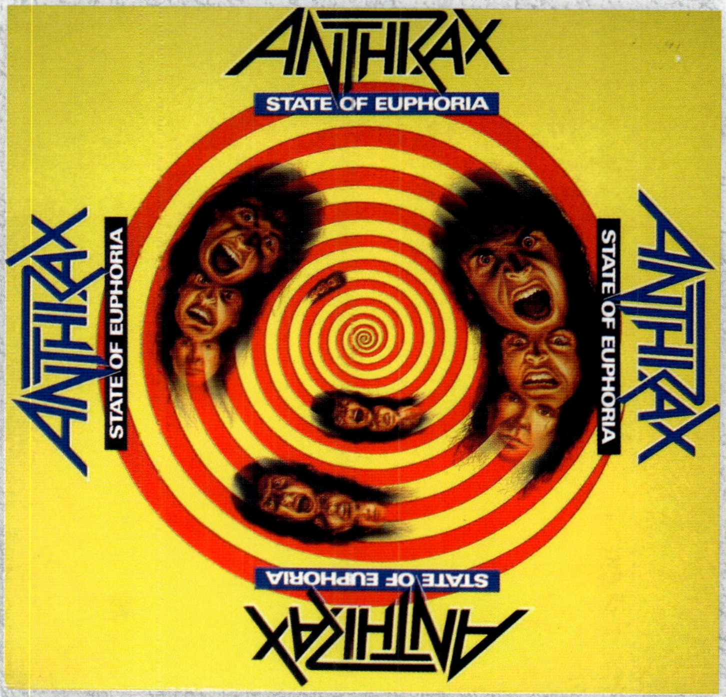

"STATE OF EUPHORIA IS WITHOUT A DOUBT ANTHRAX'S FINEST WORK TO DATE . . . 'FINALE' IS POSSIBLY ANTHRAX'S BEST EVER . . . A FITTING CLIMAX TO THE YEAR'S BEST RELEASE SO FAR."

—Bernard Doe, *Metal Forces*

Frank Bello of Anthrax leaps skyward in May 1989 in Poughkeepsie, New York, on the *State of Euphoria* tour.

1989: AND THE GRAMMY GOES TO... JETHRO TULL

Metallica started 1989 by doing something their most diehard fans believed they would never do. They made a music video. It was for the somber antiwar song "One," and it was equally as gloomy as the song, interspersing black-and-white performance footage with scenes from the 1971 movie *Johnny Got His Gun*.

One month after its debut, on February 22, 1989, Metallica appeared on the Grammy Awards. The National Academy of Recording Arts & Sciences had just created a category for hard rock and heavy metal, so having Metallica perform made perfect sense, since they were not only nominated but heavily favored to win.

After their performance of "One" for the tuxedoed luminaries in attendance, emcee Billy Crystal mock-coughed on the dry ice. Ha ha. Then Alice Cooper and Lita Ford came out to present the award that Metallica would surely get.

They announced the five nominees: AC/DC's *Blow Up Your Video*, Jane's Addiction's *Nothing's Shocking*, Jethro Tull's *Crest of a Knave*, Metallica's *. . . And Justice for All*, and Iggy Pop's *Cold Metal*. Upon opening the envelope and seeing the winner's name, Ford looked sick to her stomach.

"Jethro Tull," she announced.

Metallica was backstage, still toweling off from their performance, but nobody from the winning band was at the Shrine Auditorium. They were all back home across the pond. They had assumed Metallica would win, just like everyone else.

Tull front man Ian Anderson told *Ultimate Classic Rock* in 2012 he didn't consider *Crest of a Knave* to be a hard rock or heavy metal album. So why did they win the award in the first place? "They gave us the award because we were a bunch of nice guys who never won a Grammy before," the flautist replied.

The year was 1981, and Jethro Tull's Ian Anderson—the man upon whom the Grammys bestowed the honor of 1989's greatest heavy metal flautist—played the flute.

In 2014, Ulrich confirmed to *Rolling Stone* that everyone assumed Metallica would coast to victory that evening. The record company was so certain that it printed 10,000 promotional one-sheets for record stores declaring *. . . And Justice for All* the "Grammy Award Winner."

"We said, why don't we just put a sticker on them that says, 'Grammy Award Loser'?" Ulrich said.

Jokes aside, he could see what it meant for Metallica to perform and be nominated, even if they didn't win. Who could have imagined Metallica on the Grammys just one year earlier? He said just getting the airtime sent a powerful message. "It was sort of the first time the Grammys had said, 'Yes, there is stuff that's edgier,'" he said. "That was the real victory that day."

Slayer was also being seen by more people than ever and making themselves known outside the thrash metal underground. In 1989, *SPIN* did a long-form feature titled "Desperately Seeking Satan," in which born-again Christian evangelist Bob Larson was put on their tour bus to observe and report upon their tour in Germany. Watching the audience that the band lovingly referred to as "German vermin" sing along to "Necrophiliac," Larson observed, "They all said 'fucking' on cue. Did they know they were singing about doing it to a corpse?"

Larson may have been there to expose the scourge of Satanism, but the article went into great detail about what life on the road was like for Slayer at this point in their career. It didn't sound terrible. "Slayer's bus was a bland bus, although a luxurious one," he wrote. "Two TVs. Two VCRs. A supply of videos, mostly horror flicks. A john (number one only, please). A microwave to cook the after-concert catered meals. A center lounge (where a lot of drinking and beer-belching goes on). And in the back, bunks."

The band spent every night on the bus from midnight to six in the morning on overnight drives to the next city. It was crowded and bumpy, and Larson made a lot of jokes about how these minions of Satan should at least tour in a private jet in exchange for the eternal souls they had sold him.

Despite having a successful record and well-attended concerts, Slayer didn't have a lot of money to throw around. Larson described their status as "medium," and his description of that status suggested they had moved beyond the point of playing in a club that still had damage from a car plowing into it.

"Delectable goodies are laid out individually in the dressing room," Larson said. "Beer is there all day long, everywhere. Before going onstage, they receive a delivery from the nearest McDonald's. . . . After the show, it's a three-course dinner on real china."

Larson was also surprised to learn that no one in the band took the occult seriously. King told him he had tried to read the *Satanic Bible* but succumbed to boredom before he could make much of a dent in it. Hanneman characterized religion as "stupid" and found the whole satanic thing laughable. Lombardo said he was just there to play drums. Araya was willing to be more nuanced about it but ultimately wouldn't say whether he was a Satanist or not.

James Hetfield of Metallica informs London's Wembley Arena that he's just like a wartime novelty.

Seeking a cartoonish devotion to Satan from Slayer and its fans, Larson seemed disappointed not to find it. He even said they didn't seem interested in groupies, describing the few women who braved Slayer concerts as "slightly used and very diseased."

Finally, he observed that above all else, Slayer treasured their relationship with their fans. "They take time for autographs, photos, and small talk," he observed. "They want German vermin to know they care about their devotion."

David Fricke observed something similar when he covered Metallica's 1989 concert in Sheffield for *Rolling Stone*. After the two-hour performance, they didn't slink off to the safety of the tour bus, but rather spent the next ninety minutes signing autographs and taking photos with beaming fans.

Hetfield explained that as a young metal fan, he had found it unacceptable that some bands wouldn't mingle with fans after the show. Making sure this happened after every Metallica show mattered to him and to the band.

"If they want my autograph, that's cool," Hetfield said. "We know where they're coming from, because we've been there."

Ian reported that Anthrax had the same frenzied type of 1989 as Slayer and Metallica. "I spent so much of 1988 and 1989 on the road or recording with the band that I was never in New York," he said.

The guitarist felt the band had phoned in *State of Euphoria* and he didn't want that experience to replicate itself on their next record. Furthermore, he could tell that many bands were starting to stagnate. He didn't want the same thing to happen to them, so it was very important that the next record show they had plenty of fresh ideas. "If we didn't do something bigger and better, people were going to get bored," he said.

With that in mind, as songwriting got underway, Ian was determined to break new ground and show that Anthrax was not stuck in 1987. The next record had to show growth, and it certainly couldn't be rushed to the finish line to meet tour commitments. It needed to be a great album, and nothing could be left to chance.

ABOVE: Metallica cofounders James Hetfield and Lars Ulrich at California's Irvine Meadows Amphitheater on September 22, 1989. OPPOSITE: Kirk Hammett performs on Metallica's *Damaged Justice* tour on September 10, 1989, in Chandler, Arizona. Less than a year earlier, they performed twenty miles away in Phoenix, but they had no problem filling seats in Chandler.

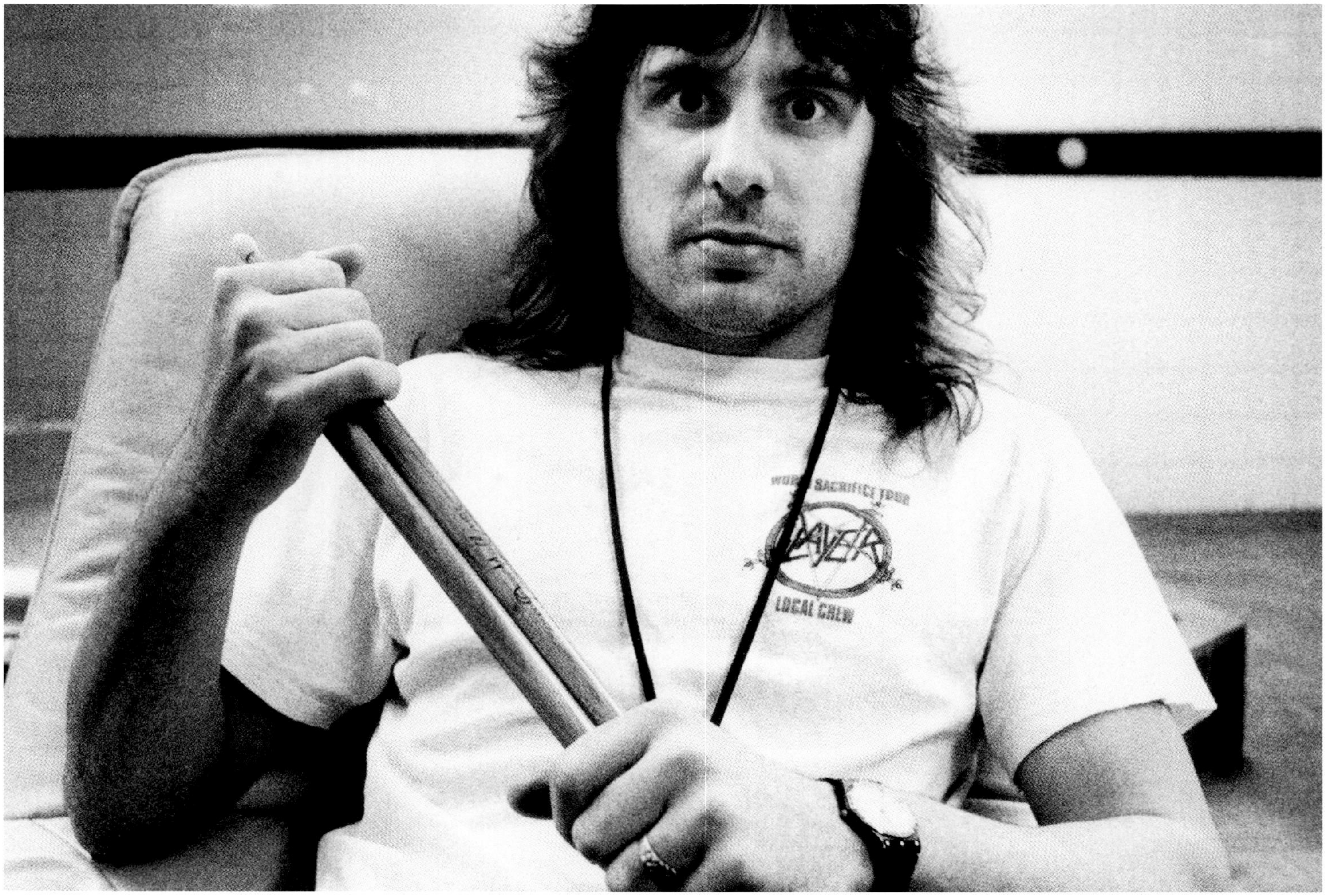

Slayer drummer Dave Lombardo wins a staring contest with the photographer at Maaspoort in the Netherlands on January 27, 1989, during the *World Sacrifice* tour.

The band went into its customary preproduction mode. Benante wrote the majority of the music, while Bello and Ian worked with him on the arrangements. Then it was time to start working on vocals.

Ian said he and Bello worked with Belladonna for a few weeks to get the vocals right, which had been their standard approach, the one that had resulted in *Among the Living*, and while it was less effective on *State of Euphoria*, he chalked that up to the rushed nature of the recording. They were resolved to take their time with this one and get it right.

Unfortunately, that wasn't the issue this time around. They said they were not getting what they needed out of Belladonna. Ian felt that the singer's approach didn't match either the more serious lyrics or the darker tone of the music they were writing. "Our usual process with Joey wasn't working anymore," he said.

Slayer (*from left*: Dave Lombardo, Kerry King, Jeff Hanneman, and Tom Araya), clearly overjoyed to be taking publicity photos.

As frustrating as that was, at least they were keeping busy. This contrasted sharply with the year Megadeth was having. They did not play a single concert in all of 1989, something that's hard to fathom for a band that spent so much time on the road.

Despite leaving the Monsters of Rock tour in 1988 to go into treatment, Ellefson said he was still using and going in and out of rehab. The band had produced a handful of demos for its next album, but otherwise, he said he spent 1989 being an addict.

At one point, he got a real surprise: a phone call from Aerosmith's Steven Tyler. The singer had gotten sober in recent years and was now providing a wellness check for a fellow recovering addict. He remembered what he was thinking as he listened to Tyler's hard-won wisdom. "I have to hurry him up and get him off the phone so my drug dealer can call me," Ellefson thought.

According to the official Megadeth website, Nick Menza became the band's new drummer that July. Ironically, he got the job the same way the guy before him had gotten his. Behler had been Samuelson's drum tech, and Menza had done the same job for Behler. Mustaine said the *So Far, So Good . . . So What!* drummer was sometimes too impaired to play, which led Menza through the same tech-to-drummer pipeline.

The band's website only lists two other notable events in 1989, both of which took place that October. The first was recording Alice Cooper's "No More Mr. Nice Guy" for the soundtrack to Wes Craven's *Shocker*. This necessitated a music video, which was overseen by Penelope Spheeris, who famously observed that Mustaine showed up for the shoot impaired, which made her job quite difficult. That's really something, considering she's worked with children and dogs.

Charlie Benante of Anthrax holds court in May 1989 on the *State of Euphoria* tour.

Mustaine did not dispute her account. He noted that he was standing on a rotating, seesawing platform, which would have been difficult even if his bloodstream had contained nothing but the natural endorphins produced by exercise. The platform he referred to is not shown in the video, since he's shot from the waist up, so this may not have been readily apparent to viewers. That disclaimer aside, he endorsed her account. "I was basically too fucked up to play guitar at my usual level on the day of the shoot," he said.

The other major event noted on the Megadeth website for October 1989 is "Mustaine is arrested for impaired driving, forced to clean up in 12-step program." In his memoir, he listed "marijuana, Valium, cocaine, heroin, chloral hydrate . . . alcohol, a spoon, and a syringe" as things that authorities "found in my blood or in my car" when he was pulled over on Ventura Boulevard.

Saying he was "forced to clean up" oversells it a bit. He acknowledged being ordered by the legal system to go into recovery and enroll in a diversion program, but it did not result in sobriety, in part because he was paying Ellefson to go to AA meetings for him.

He was a long way from exacting the revenge he had once vowed to visit upon Metallica. While Mustaine was contending with court-ordered rehab, his former band was featured in *Rolling Stone* and was being treated like the Next Big Thing. The article featured a quote from Metal Blade's Brian Slagel, who credited them with thrash metal's breakthrough and success. "When they came out, there was no speed metal or thrash metal," Slagel said. "They were doing something new."

The article featured Ozzy Osbourne, who said Metallica were young and hungry, like Black Sabbath in 1970. It featured Newsted, saying people would still be listening to Metallica in twenty years, like Led Zeppelin. All of that could have applied to Megadeth as well, since they had their own distinct sound and had become successful on their own terms. But it was Metallica receiving the kudos, and worst of all, it referred to "Metallica and its chief contemporaries, Anthrax, Megadeth, and Slayer."

Anthrax and Slayer may have appreciated the mention, but it's easy to imagine that same phrase sending Mustaine into paroxysms of blind rage. He did not want to just be a chief contemporary, so if he still wanted Megadeth to succeed and Metallica to fail, he would have to make some changes. Otherwise, his band would always be an also-ran forever in Metallica's shadow.

ABOVE: Frank Bello and Joey Belladonna of Anthrax being brave and mighty in May 1989 on the *State of Euphoria* tour. LEFT: Anthrax (*from left*: Frank Bello, Joey Belladonna, Dan Spitz, Charlie Benante, and Scott Ian) in 1989, when thrash metal was ascendant and shifting units.

LEFT: Metallica bassist Jason Newsted at Irvine Meadows Amphitheater on September 23, 1989, the third and final night of their engagement there. OPPOSITE: Grammy award losers Metallica (*from left*: James Hetfield, Lars Ulrich, Jason Newsted, and Kirk Hammett).

FAITH NO MORE

THE BIG FOUR VS. HEADBANGERS BALL

THRASH METAL WAS not embraced by MTV in 1987. It would be more accurate to say that MTV reluctantly resigned itself to acknowledging it, moaning and complaining the whole time. The genre was gaining popularity and visibility, so MTV sighed, shrugged, and began airing the handful of existing thrash metal videos on a new show called *Headbangers Ball*. Polite society still considered the music a blight, but it was popular enough to force MTV's hand.

The show premiered on April 18, 1987, and aired on Saturday nights from midnight to 2 a.m. The Big Four bands all acknowledge that appearing on the show helped get their names out there, and Ian said that when Anthrax's video for "Antisocial" went into heavy rotation, it undeniably helped shift units. You hate to give MTV credit for anything, but that was just a fact.

Metallica inarguably saw the most bang for their buck by making a video for "One." Directed by Bill Pope and Michael Salomon, it debuted on MTV on January 20, 1989, at 3:30 in the morning on the West Coast. Salomon said in *Metal Hammer* in 2022 that he didn't have high expectations for it. MTV was still chilly to thrash metal, and he wasn't sure it would get played much.

"A week after it aired, MTV had so many requests that they started playing it in daytime, among Michael Jackson and Bon Jovi videos," he said. The pile-on had begun, and record companies started sending every thrash band on their rosters out to make a video.

Slayer was sent to Cairo to film the video for the title track to their 1990 album, *Seasons in the Abyss*. It's safe to say that was not cheap, and King told *Metal Forces* in 1991 that he didn't expect videos to do much for them. "They're a waste of money," he said. "I mean, a couple of plays on the *Headbangers Ball* and that's it."

Araya said Rubin told the band to do it. The producer had received assurances that it would get played, but once it was delivered to the network, whoops! They lost it under the sofa or something. "They hardly show it at all," the bassist said. "We'll never spend that kind of money on a promo video again."

Of all the Big Four music videos, Megadeth enjoys the distinction of making one of the stupidest of all time, "Hangar 18." The performance footage is all fine and good, but it's interspersed with a depiction of a sadistic medical experiment being performed on a poor extraterrestrial specimen, created with a less convincing puppet than the one in *ALF*. But again, units were shifted.

Thrash fans tuned in to *Headbangers Ball* every week, despite knowing perfectly well that they might see one thrash video in the entire two hours if they were lucky. Indeed, they suffered power ballad upon power ballad in the hopes that there might be an Exodus video. It was customary to invite friends over to drink crappy domestic beer, do bong hits, and complain about how much the show sucked while waiting for such a video to come on.

This ritual would conclude with the program airing a single thrash metal video at 1:55 a.m. The credits would roll and fans would conclude that MTV sucked and so did the show. Then, one week later, all those same malcontents would show up at the same house to watch the next episode.

Ellefson said in his memoir that thrash metal bands were ultimately rejected by MTV as abruptly as the network had initially embraced them. "All of a sudden, MTV was very clearly not playing heavy metal videos," he wrote. "Mainstream music channels were simply not going to play our videos anymore."

He rightly recognized that, as tough as that treatment had been, the real Megadeth fans were still out there and still paying attention. MTV had been interested in the band in a superficial way only for as long as it suited them, but when the network unceremoniously ghosted them, the same fans who had put them over the top, and who would watch the show every week in the hopes of seeing their favorite band (which they never did), were still there.

"That is the power of heavy metal and our fans," Ellefson said. MTV may have been fickle, but the fans were ride-or-die. Still, Ellefson said the brief union of Megadeth and MTV wasn't completely worthless and acknowledged the value it had brought to them. "MTV had taken us from being a band that played five-hundred-seat clubs to arenas through sheer exposure," he said.

Fans of thrash metal and *schadenfreude* ultimately got the last laugh. MTV stopped broadcasting its dedicated music channels on December 31, 2025, the result of a sweeping edict from the parent company, Paramount Skydance. Just as MTV had shown formerly popular artists the door the second they believed it would profit them to do so, its parent company was now unceremoniously flushing it down the same toilet. One can only hope that whoever made the decision to stop airing thrash metal videos was tearfully escorted from their offices by security guards in a very public, humiliating way, and hopefully it was filmed. Karma's a bitch.

Host Riki Rachtman of MTV's *Headbangers Ball* guides viewers through two hours of music videos whose decent-to-insufferable ratio was 1:25 on a good night.

Megadeth 3.0. Drummer Nick Menza and guitarist Marty Friedman join the Daves (seated) to create what some fans consider their greatest era.

CHAPTER 10

1990: RUST NEVER SLEEPS

Megadeth's fortunes began to improve in 1990. Mustaine was in manager Ron Laffitte's office in February and spotted a record on his desk called *Dragon's Kiss* by Shrapnel Records artist Marty Friedman. To those not in the know, Shrapnel specialized in "shred," an extremely technical and very fast style of lead guitar, and Friedman was one of its foremost purveyors.

Laffitte played it for Mustaine, and he was sold before the first song ended. He didn't merely like what he heard—he was truly bowled over by it and had to have this guy in the band. Friedman's audition sealed it. "He understood the nuances of our music and played the songs perfectly," Ellefson said.

While Friedman's technique alone was more than enough to win him the gig, he was also an established musician with his own fanbase. The shred audience was not massive, and the genre would never go mainstream, but he had a dedicated following who loved what he did, and that brought a lot of value to Megadeth when he joined.

Early in 1990, another event changed things. Ellefson got sober and stayed sober. He said it was amusing to enter the recording studio in a lucid state, as the songs they would be recording for the upcoming album were written while he and Mustaine were, in his words, "completely out of our minds on very hard drugs."

Mustaine had gotten clean, too, and said Alice Cooper was instrumental in that. He had made himself available to Mustaine the same way Steven Tyler had made himself available to Ellefson, but when he and Cooper spoke on the phone, unlike Ellefson, he didn't try to keep the line open for his dealer. Rather, he said three words to Cooper that had been a long time coming: "I need help."

Sober Megadeth entered the studio that spring, decamping to Rumbo Recorders, owned by Daryl Dragon and his wife, Toni, better known as Captain and Tennille of "Love Will Keep Us Together" fame. The album would bear the title *Rust in Peace*, based on a bumper sticker Mustaine saw expressing the hope that all nuclear weapons would do exactly that.

RIGHT: A sober Dave Mustaine in 1990. Fun fact: The legendary Alice Cooper not only helped Mustaine get sober but also became the Megadeth guitarist's godfather. OPPOSITE: Dave Mustaine and Marty Friedman of Megadeth, whose six-string chops were so prodigious their songs could support up to eleven guitar solos a pop.

The recording was executed with surgical precision, and the tempos were taken at dangerous speeds. The album would go on to be their highest charting yet, hitting #23. It sold more than one million copies and even earned a Grammy nomination. Megadeth had emerged from its year in the wilderness stronger and more popular than ever.

But money was still an issue. Ellefson said that sobriety enabled him to meaningfully dig into the band's finances, which taught him how the music business operated. For the first time, he saw how the sausage was made, to borrow an expression. It was easy to make a popular album, go out on a sold-out tour, and still earn next to nothing. In fact, after the managers and agents took their cut, you could lose money. Labels loaned bands money to record, tour, and make videos, and they expected bands to recoup those loans. If they spent a million dollars on your video, your album better sell enough to make it back.

"It doesn't work like that in any other business," he said, opining that even McDonald's gave its teenage employees more of a fair shake. While he acknowledged that he had wasted every cent he had earned from Megadeth's first three albums all by himself, it was still a rude awakening to discover that this legal chicanery was enshrined in the recording contract Megadeth had put their signatures to.

There wasn't a lot of time to dwell on it. *Rust in Peace* was in stores and it was time to support it on the road. The group embarked on the *Clash of the Titans* tour alongside Slayer. It was a little awkward, since there had been hostilities between his band and the Slayer guys.

In 1991, Bernard Doe of *Metal Forces* asked about the origin of the Megadeth-Slayer beef. After all, they were both from the same area, and King had even been in Megadeth for a few gigs. Why can't we all get along? King revealed that he didn't have a problem with the band. He only had a problem with one member, and it wasn't David Ellefson, Marty Friedman, or Nick Menza. It was the founding member he had issues with.

"He's a miserable son of a bitch, nobody wants to be around him, and whenever you are, he makes it a point of making you feel miserable, regardless of who you are," he said.

Regardless, the tour was a good opportunity for Slayer, and they grabbed it. They had a new album to promote, called *Seasons in the Abyss*, and like Megadeth, they, too, had expenses to recoup. The label had insisted on a video for the title track, which featured the band performing in front of the Pyramids of Giza in Egypt. For a band that had built itself from the ground up while MTV did nothing to help, it was galling to throw so much money at an effort meant to accommodate the network. They understood that music videos were a necessity, but it pissed them off that making back that money was now their problem.

While there may have been concerns about how Megadeth and Slayer would get along on tour, Ellefson said the number-one priority was keeping him and Mustaine sober. The tour managers were instructed to ensure there was no alcohol in any hotel room minibar, and they had their own dedicated security guard whose entire job was to keep the Daves away from any judgment-impairing substances that might materialize.

The bill was rounded out by Testament and Suicidal Tendencies, both of whom had new albums out and were seeing increased success of their own as thrash metal became more popular. Those two bands were never as commercially successful as the Big Four, but even being adjacent to them was helpful. Everyone got to bask in the glow.

Around the same time, Anthrax was encountering a challenge of their own. Early in 1990, a fire at their rehearsal space destroyed half their equipment. It could have taken more had the band and some friends not made a human chain from the practice room window to the roof and then to the ground.

Public Enemy (*from left*: Professor Griff, an S1W security member, Flavor Flav, Terminator X, Chuck D, and another S1W member), whose music was so beloved by some members of Anthrax that the band eventually covered "Bring the Noise."

While anyone who owns beloved musical equipment would see this as a rational act, they did it against the advice of the fire department. Also rational was Ian's decision to keep one of the affected guitars, a Flying V, even though it had suffered some damage. "The pickguard and knobs were partially melted because it was close to where the fire was, but it looked super cool," he said. "I just left them on there."

The band decamped to Los Angeles to begin making the next record. Tracking went well and all the instrumentation went to tape exactly as the band wanted. They had created an instrumental bed for the songs that was darker and more menacing than anything that bore their name before, which Benante told the *Aquarian* in 2015 was a by-product of recent travails. "We were going through a lot of shit at that time," he said.

The situation with Belladonna remained. The guy could unquestionably sing, so there was nothing wrong there, but Ian had written much more serious lyrics this time around and felt the singer's approach was not appropriate for the subject matter. He began discussing the situation in secret with his other bandmates, laying the groundwork for a big change.

When they were done tracking, he had an idea he wanted to explore. Rap had gotten bigger in the handful of years since "I'm the Man," and there had been overlap between genres when "Angel of Death" was sampled by an ascendant group called Public Enemy for their song "She Watch Channel Zero." It appeared on their 1988 album *It Takes a Nation of Millions to Hold Us Back*, which was harder, rawer, and more political than other rap records on the *Billboard* charts. Metal wasn't the only changing genre.

"Scott and I just loved Public Enemy," *Twin Peaks* fan Benante told the *Twin Peaks Archive* in 2008. "To us, Public Enemy was the epitome of what rap is."

Public Enemy appeared on the *Less Than Zero* soundtrack alongside Slayer, contributing a track called "Bring the Noise." Ian was such a fan, he decided Anthrax should cover it, then send the tape to Public Enemy's Chuck D and Flavor Flav to do the vocals. It didn't hurt that the rap group had mentioned Anthrax in the original "Bring the Noise," and the drummer said that their own version was meant to be a kind of "back atcha" for name-checking them.

Ian and Benante laid down their tracks in just a few minutes, the telltale sign that a band has something on their hands. After Bello laid down his bass, they sent the instrumental track to Chuck D. The response was exactly what Anthrax had hoped for.

"I remember sending the track to Chuck, and he called me up to say how much he loved it," the drummer said. "In his exact words, 'This track is slammin'!'"

Despite the cover being listed as a collaboration, no one from Public Enemy ever came into the studio to add vocals. Instead, Anthrax used the original recording's vocals and painstakingly overlaid them on the Anthrax bed track, word by word, without the benefit of sampling technology to smooth the process. Today, a twelve-year-old with a laptop could do the same thing in ten minutes, but in 1990, it was an all-analog process that took forever.

Anthrax released *Persistence of Time* in August, just before Slayer and Megadeth went out on the *Clash of the Titans* tour. Ian had been so excited by their cover of "Bring the Noise" that he was already thinking of going out on tour with Public Enemy, but they had dates booked with Iron Maiden in the fall. Ian said that five weeks into the tour, Maiden singer Bruce Dickinson lost his voice, leading to the cancelation of ten shows. "We were stuck and bleeding money," Ian said.

LEFT: Frank Bello and a newly mustachioed Dan Spitz of Anthrax keep it in the family in the 1990s. OPPOSITE: The members of Anthrax felt that singer Joey Belladonna's performance on the 1990 Persistence of Time album did not spark joy, so he was later replaced by Armored Saint's John Bush (top left).

Kellogg's
FLAKES

Slayer (*from left*: Tom Araya, Jeff Hanneman, Kerry King, and Dave Lombardo) in Genk, Belgium, on September 22, 1990, during the *Clash of the Titans* tour. Megadeth's Dave Mustaine did not care for their sophomoric shenanigans during this tour.

Their crew got paid whether the band performed or not, and they also lost money on hotel reservations in ten cities. At the tour's end, Anthrax was $80,000 in the red. Absent going into sex work or selling their internal organs on the black market, there was no way they could come up with even a fraction of that money. It might as well have been a trillion dollars.

At the end of the tour, the band tried to address the massive debt, only to be informed that they owed nothing. Iron Maiden and their manager, Rod Smallwood, had made up the entire loss for them. "They're some of the best guys you could ever hope to meet," Ian said of Maiden.

Metallica, meanwhile, was trying to figure out their next move, although not in parallel with the other three bands. Those guys were all on tour, but Metallica was holed up in the studio—it would be quite a while before they came out. They had graduated to the next level with . . . *And Justice for All*, but the members agreed that the songs were too long, too complex, and a chore to perform live.

They had changed with every album and they wanted to do something that was not a sequel to . . . *And Justice for All*, even though it was then the most successful album in their catalog. They were never in the sequel business, and they believed every new album should take a fresh approach. But in the wake of this one-off mutation, what did that look like?

"After *Justice* . . . it was pretty apparent that we needed some guidance," Hetfield told *Louder* in 2022. That guidance came in the form of Mötley Crüe producer Bob Rock. According to *Metallica: The $24.95 Book* by Ben Apatoff, Hetfield and Ulrich were eager to simplify their music, and while they weren't interested in making music that was "Mötley Crüe simple," they were interested in something that was "AC/DC simple." They believed Rock was the person to get them there.

They enlisted him for their next record, making a subset of hardcore fans particularly unhappy. In fact, some never recovered and will take that grudge to their graves. After all, Metallica and the other Big Four bands were formed to act as the loyal opposition to glam metal, and now here they were, hiring the man who had produced the last Mötley Crüe album.

It was nothing less than utter heresy.

1981 1982 1983 1984 1985 1986

ANTHRAX WAS EASILY THE GOOFIEST OF THE BIG FOUR BANDS, AN IMAGE THEY CONSCIOUSLY CULTIVATED. BUT ON PERSISTENCE OF TIME, THEY WERE SERIOUS AS CANCER.

OPPOSITE: Metallica (*from left*: James Hetfield, Kirk Hammett, Lars Ulrich, and Jason Newsted) are dressed to the nines—or at least dressed up enough for a job interview at Guitar Center.

REVIEW

ANTHRAX

Persistence of Time

PERSISTENCE OF TIME was an important record for Anthrax. *State of Euphoria* was just not up to snuff, so the 1990 record had to prove the band wasn't out of ideas. It was a new decade, and the band was determined to move forward.

They were easily the goofiest of the Big Four bands, an image they consciously cultivated. *Mad* magazine cartoonist Mort Drucker had drawn a caricature of them for the back cover of the previous album, and they showed a lot of humor in their music and lyrics. But on *Persistence of Time*, they were serious as cancer.

Right from the opener, "Time," you can tell the band is determined to get it right this time and make something they could vouch for. While saying something is a "return to form" can be a backhanded compliment, it applies here, and the band also ventures into new territory that may have surprised fans at the time.

The band was dissatisfied with Belladonna's performance on the album, claiming his approach didn't match the music. Honestly, if you didn't know the band members felt that way, you would never know it was an issue. Maybe there are a couple of moments here and there that fall flat, but overall, it's hard to tell what the problem was.

The peak of the album is an eleven-minute stretch that starts with "Intro to Reality," segues into "Belly of the Beast," and ends with the Joe Jackson cover, "Got the Time." They seem to be covering it not as a gag, but as an enthusiastic tribute to a song they really like. "'Got the Time' is such a great song," longtime Joe Jackson fan Benante told *Eon Music* in 2021.

Unfortunately, *Persistence of Time* has the same problem plaguing previous Anthrax records: The songs are simply too long. "Blood" and "Keep It in the Family" just don't need to be seven minutes each, and as the second and third songs on the record, they create a fourteen-minute obstacle for listeners to overcome. It's not a deal-breaker, but you may find yourself checking to see how much of each song is left.

THIS RECORD IS PRETTY MUCH ALL ABOUT GUITAR SOLOS, AND IT LANDED FRIEDMAN AND MUSTAINE ON THE COVER OF EVERY MAGAZINE EVER PUBLISHED FOR ASPIRING SIX-STRINGERS.

REVIEW

MEGADETH

Rust in Peace

WRITTEN IMPAIRED AND recorded sober, *Rust in Peace* was the first Megadeth album to feature Marty Friedman and Nick Menza in a lineup many fans believe represents the band at its peak.

There was certainly no way anyone could say these guys were crappy guitar players. Friedman was arguably Mustaine's most effective sparring partner, and his style was distinct from that of the band's founder. As a pair, they were at a completely different level than most of their thrash contemporaries, none of whom were slouches themselves. Ellefson and Menza turn in epic performances, but this record is pretty much all about guitar solos, and it landed Friedman and Mustaine on the cover of every magazine ever published for aspiring six-stringers.

"Hangar 18" features a jaw-dropping eleven guitar solos in its approximately five-minute duration. Molly Hatchet doesn't even have that many. But unlike some twin-guitar teams that simply take turns soloing, Friedman and Mustaine respond to each other's leads while also trying to one-up each other. They were thrash metal's answer to Thin Lizzy's Scott Gorham and Brian Robertson.

"Holy Wars . . . the Punishment Due" displays everyone's chops to impressive effect from the second it starts. The riff in the opening is deadly, and the melodic figure starting at the forty-five-second mark winds its catchy way directly into the ear canal, never to emerge again. It stays stuck in your head forever. In 2008, *Digital Dream Door* ranked Friedman's solo on "Tornado of Souls" as the fourth-greatest metal guitar solo in history.

A year later, *Kerrang!* put *Rust in Peace* at the top of their "Where to Start with . . ." listing for Megadeth, calling it an "essential purchase": "An album that has since gone on to act as a makeshift bible to almost any aspiring guitar players, *Rust in Peace* features several of the band's most triumphant moments, sealing its reputation as one of thrash metal's most genuinely classic offerings."

REVIEW

SLAYER

Seasons in the Abyss

SEASONS IN THE ABYSS heralded something wonderful for Slayer. Namely, they didn't have to follow *Reign in Blood*. *South of Heaven* (1988) had done all that heavy lifting; now they could just put a new record out and not worry about beating, topping, or repudiating anything.

Of course, everything Slayer ever recorded from 1988 on was met with the question, "Is it as good as *Reign in Blood*? Is it faster? Does it have enough Satanism?" As preoccupied as some fans may have been with those matters, the band seemed cool with moving on, which means there are some slow and midtempo things on the album in addition to the fast stuff.

But fret not! There is high-speed stuff on *Seasons in the Abyss*, which is apparent from the opening track, "War Ensemble." "Spirit in Black," "Hallowed Point," and "Born of Fire" also do their level best to break the sound barrier. That's not to say, however, that the slower stuff isn't good—"Blood Red," the quite disturbing "Dead Skin Mask," and the title track all take Slayer into new areas that may not be fast but are crunchy as hell nonetheless.

Sadly, as with *South of Heaven*, *Seasons in the Abyss* fails to replicate *Reign in Blood*'s zero-tolerance policy toward filler. "Expendable Youth" and "Skeletons of Society" are, plainly put, dull. They're both under five minutes, so the damage is limited, but they drag down the overall listening experience a bit.

Seasons in the Abyss was the final Slayer album before drummer Dave Lombardo was replaced by Paul Bostaph of Forbidden. He returned for the 2006 album, *Christ Illusion*, and his tenure lasted long enough for him to participate in the 2010 and 2011 Big Four concerts.

Sadly, Lombardo eventually parted ways with the band in an incredibly acrimonious split, and between that and the 2013 death of guitarist Jeff Hanneman, the *Reign in Blood* lineup went the way of Metallica's *Master of Puppets* lineup. The men who helped give the world "Angel of Death" and "Orion"—the most brutal and progressive pillars of the thrash metal movement—were gone.

OF COURSE, EVERYTHING SLAYER EVER RECORDED FROM 1988 ON WAS MET WITH THE QUESTION, "IS IT AS GOOD AS REIGN IN BLOOD? IS IT FASTER? DOES IT HAVE ENOUGH SATANISM?"

Dave Mustaine and Nick Menza of Megadeth during the *Clash of the Titans* tour. Mustaine would later say this Megadeth lineup was "on fire."

CHAPTER 11

1991: CLASH OF THE TITANS

Megadeth started the spring of 1991 with a short European tour. More dates had been booked for the summer's North American leg of Clash of the Titans, but the spring outing was an opportunity for a quick hit before that got underway. Their openers were Seattle newcomers Alice in Chains, whom they saw for the first time opening for them in Zürich. "We were blown away," Ellefson told the *Network317 Podcast* in 2020.

Fortuitously, the upcoming leg of Clash of the Titans still needed an opening band. Death Angel had been set to do it, but unfortunately were involved in a serious tour bus accident and had to pull out. This allowed Alice in Chains to open the 1991 leg of the *Clash of the Titans* tour, which resumed on May 16, 1991, in Dallas.

Megadeth and Slayer were back for more, but where Testament had been the third band, allowing Megadeth and Slayer to alternate headlining slots, they were joined on the tour by Anthrax instead. Three bands from the Big Four were touring together for the first time, and Ellefson told *Ultimate Guitar* in 2019 that, even at that point, Metallica's name was being thrown around. "We were known even back then as the Big Four," he noted.

Having Metallica on the tour would have made sense in that respect, but at that point in 1991, they were still finishing their next record. In 2010, King told *Guitar World* it was unlikely that Metallica would have participated at the time anyway. "There might have even been talk of a *Big Four* tour back then, but we probably couldn't get Metallica onboard," he said.

With Anthrax, Slayer, and Megadeth, the bands opted for a rotating, co-headlining lineup. The bands would alternate who would open, who would close, and who would get sandwiched in the middle. What could possibly go wrong?

"That was the beginning of me and Dave Mustaine being at odds, because he was just a pompous ass back then," King said.

At issue was Mustaine's interview account of the Slayer guys. He described them as drunken and boorish, which is not hard to picture. In 2010, he clarified that at the time he was newly sober and in "AA police" mode. More to the point, he knew if he hung out with them, he could relapse.

"I saw those guys having fun, and I just wanted to be with them and hang out, but I knew if I did that, I would probably drink," he said. "I was suffering silently, my lips gave way, and I spoke out.

BELOW: The late, great Nick Menza, who pounded the skins for Megadeth and did so quite admirably. Listen to his playing on *Rust in Peace* if you're skeptical. The guy just killed it. OPPOSITE: Alice in Chains (*from left*: Jerry Cantrell, Layne Staley, Mike Starr, and Sean Kinney) got a huge break when they were added to the *Clash of the Titans* tour. Thrash fans threw garbage (and worse) at them during their sets, but they stayed onstage no matter what. Respect.

Tom Araya of Slayer awaits the hour of reprisal during the *Seasons in the Abyss* tour on January 18, 1991, in Denver, Colorado.

I said something about Kerry that I shouldn't have said, and that I regretted. . . . It's water under the bridge now."

King remembered the incident, and in 2010, he said he was amused by it more than anything else. Clearly, he saw it as water under the bridge, too. "I remember reading an interview where he said that he was angry about us drinking in the hallways, farting and burping, and having a good time," he said. "I'm like, 'You're just making us sound fun, dude.'"

You know who wasn't having any fun? Alice in Chains. The Anthrax, Megadeth, and Slayer fans in attendance did not care for the moody Pacific Northwest sound of this new band, and they let them know it by throwing trash at them throughout their entire set. A decade earlier, fans of older, more established bands thought thrash metal was just stupid noise and rejected it. Now, it was thrash metal's turn to be bitterly averse to the change these new young whippersnappers were foisting on everyone.

"Alice in Chains had a fucking hard time on that tour," Scott Ian told *Guitar World*. "We'd stand onstage every night and just watch them get pelted with anything and everything those crowds could throw at them."

All of the Big Four bands had paid their dues and endured audiences that didn't care for them, didn't understand them, and wanted them to just go away. They didn't, and now it was the new guys receiving that treatment. Ian said they admirably took it on the chin.

"They never once walked off the stage," he said. "Every night they finished their fucking set. They stood there, and they took it . . . it was absolutely trial by fire for them."

King observed the same thing. Despite the hostile reception, they kept playing, no matter what came their way, even including post-consumer waste, as was the case at Colorado's Red Rocks. "Somebody had a big gallon jug that they had emptied out and

Jon Zazula had advised Anthrax (*from left*: Frank Bello, Joey Belladonna, Dan Spitz, Charlie Benante, and Scott Ian) that they would make more money on their *Persistence of Time* tour if they didn't have an elaborate stage set. Oh well, you couldn't talk them out of it.

pissed in," he said. "They dumped it on Alice in Chains more than once."

When the young band left the stage, the audience stopped throwing things out of hostility and switched to throwing things out of love. On one date, they threw clumps of sod at Anthrax throughout their entire set; Megadeth received the same treatment when they came onstage next. They left at the end of their set, but Araya told *The Quietus* in 2015 that an enraged Mustaine ran back out to give the audience a talking-to and reprimand them for throwing mud. He probably should have expected the response he got.

"They just started throwing more and more at him," the bassist recalled.

It didn't matter. Megadeth had not just successfully rebuilt itself, but it had come back strong enough to silence the doubters. Mustaine looked back on it fondly and remembered it as a great time to be in the band. "We were just on fire," he said. "I think that probably was the best period for Megadeth."

When the tour ended, Ian got the shock of his life. He received a call from the band's business manager, who asked where he should "send the check." The guitarist didn't understand the question, so the business manager explained that it was a check for tour profits. It had taken a full decade since the band's founding, but for the first time, Anthrax made money. Ellefson had a similar experience.

"The advances were recouped, we paid back all our debts, and I paid Dave back the remainder of a $5,000 loan he'd given me in 1989," Ellefson said.

As Clash of the Titans wrapped up, Anthrax released *Attack of the Killer B's*, a B-sides compilation that featured the newly recorded version of "Bring the Noise." It had been difficult to get it released at all, as the new regime at Island Records simply

Dan Spitz and Frank Bello of Anthrax bring noise to Philadelphia's Spectrum on June 29, 1991.

didn't get it. After Zazula threatened to release it on Megaforce and disparage Island in the process, the label let it come out. It went on to turn rap-metal into a genre unto itself, and Ian singled out Rage Against the Machine for taking what Anthrax had started and turning it into something of their own. "Rage created this whole new thing that was absolutely groundbreaking," he said.

That August, Metallica released their long-awaited follow-up to . . . *And Justice for All*. Simply called *Metallica* and featuring a flat black cover, the record debuted at #1 on the *Billboard* chart. A commercially unpalatable genre had hit the big time, and no one was more surprised than the band. "I never thought it was possible to have a number-one record with the kind of music we played," Newsted told *Rolling Stone* in 1991.

Just as MTV had been forced by market realities to put the "One" video into high rotation, the mainstream press was forced to start covering the band. This situation was best personified when *SPIN* writer Bob Mack felt compelled to give an explanatory blurb to his profile of the band: "Metallica has always been eerily popular, but never very good."

The moment recalled an observation King had made in *Metal Forces*. Slayer was receiving widespread coverage from news outlets that had previously ignored them or had even called them outright garbage. He said he knew it wasn't because critics now suddenly enjoyed the music. The publications were just acknowledging market realities. "I guess it helps them sell magazines if they pretend to like Slayer," he said.

While it would be wrong to accuse the esteemed publication known as *SPIN* of just trying to sell magazines, it sure seemed to be the case when they covered Metallica. To his credit, Mack was at least honest about why he had never liked the band. "I was spooked by the new generation of two million kids who did like them, legions of zealous misfits that I was too old to understand," he admitted.

Public Enemy and Anthrax in Chicago in June 1991 during the video shoot for "Bring the Noise." Flavor Flav, Chuck D, and Scott Ian are up front while Charlie Benante, Frank Bello, and Dan Spitz are in the back.

See? How hard was that? Mack then compared Metallica's newfound popularity to that of the Canadian band Rush. They had been more of a niche band in the 1970s but went mainstream with the 1980 release of "Spirit of Radio." This comparison prompted Ulrich to make a statement that seemed utterly bizarre at the time. "More than any other band, we are like Rush," he said.

History has vindicated this once controversial statement. Like the Canadian rockers, Metallica changed with every record, and they hit the charts not because they were chasing hits. They just happened to make music people liked. They were also like Rush in that their fanbase declared them sellouts with every new record, only to buy it and see them in concert anyway. In *Guitar World*, Hammett even gave a very Rush-like explanation for their latest stylistic shift. "We wanted to create a different record and offer something new to our audience," he said.

A lot of diehards said Metallica had sold out, but in reality they were the same people they had always been, and they hadn't changed a thing to get popular. The mainstream had simply caught up to them.

It wasn't simple getting there. The group, whom David Fricke called "the scourge of the mainstream" in *Rolling Stone*, had worked on *Metallica* for ten months and spent over $1 million by the time it was finished. During the sessions, Rock would sometimes demand forty-plus takes from the musicians, and three of the four band members entered the recording studio as married men and exited it as divorced men.

So, was it worth it?

"I've run into fans who think the album's crap," Hammett said.

Be that as it may, the stylistic shift was inevitable. Touring for *. . . And Justice for All* and playing ten-minute songs every night got old fast, for both the band and the audience. "I can remember

1981	1982	1983	1984	1985	1986

ABOVE: Release the Kraken! Dave Mustaine of Megadeth in Costa Mesa, California, on May 25, 1991, during the *Clash of the Titans* tour. OPPOSITE: An epic whoosh of ginger hair and Dave Mustaine do their thing in front of the adoring masses.

getting offstage one night after playing 'Justice' and one of us saying, 'Fuck, that's the last time we ever play that fucking song,'" Hammett said.

On September 28, shortly after the album's release, Metallica performed in Moscow at the Tushino Airfield. They were part of a Monsters of Rock package that included AC/DC and had been organized by the Russian government to thank the young citizenry for helping foil a coup attempt on August 19, literally one week after *Metallica* was released.

Crowd size estimates ranged from 150,000 to 1.6 million, but there has never been a definitive tally of how many people were actually there. Just fire up YouTube and see for yourself. It looks like the entire population of every former Soviet republic had shown up.

ROCK

ABOVE: Metallica (*from left*: Lars Ulrich, Kirk Hammett, Jason Newsted, and James Hetfield) at the MTV Video Music Awards on September 5, 1991, in Universal City, California. Clearly, a lot had changed in just a few years. OPPOSITE: It's April 21, 1991, and representatives of Anthrax, Megadeth, and Slayer (*from left*: Jeff Hanneman, Scott Ian, Kerry King, and Dave Mustaine) put aside their differences for the greater good of the photo shoot.

The night before the performance, Ulrich and Hammett went out on the town. It was a novel thing for Western artists to play in the former Soviet Union, and for Metallica, it was their first time on Russian soil. It was there that the success of their new album was put into perspective.

"I remember one kid in the hotel," Ulrich said. "He just stood there in front of me, crying. 'You don't know what it means to me for you to come here.' . . . These kids were so appreciative of the fact that we were coming there, and it was very heavy to think that maybe our music gave them a little something to grasp on to."

He said it was near the Russian White House, where three citizens had been killed in the August uprising, that he was truly affected. "They had built a tent city in this square where the kids got killed," Ulrich said. "They took us on walks around the square, showing us where the barricades were. . . . We were number one all over the rest of the world, and sitting in the square, it didn't mean dick."

The year in thrash metal ended with the release of Slayer's double live album, *Decade of Aggression*, which celebrated a literal decade of aggression. The performances were mostly culled from Clash of the Titans dates, so fans who weren't jazzed about the counterfeit audience on *Live Undead* were probably happy to get the real thing—ninety minutes of pure Slayer hysteria recorded in front of the kind of seething mob only they could attract. It didn't replicate Metallica's #1 debut, but it was still a big deal for Slayer to reach #55 on the *Billboard* charts, especially with a live album.

Around the same time, an obscure band released a new album. It debuted in the lower reaches of the Top 200, so it's easy to see why a lot of people initially overlooked it. It was called *Nevermind*, and it was by Nirvana, who, like Alice in Chains, hailed from Seattle. When it reached #1 in the new year, no one could deny that something new and refreshing was happening.

At the same time, the once-explosive new genre of thrash metal was now ten years old. Looking back, it's easy to see that a changing of the guard was in the offing, but at the time, few people noticed that the golden age of thrash metal had reached its expiration date.

REVIEW

METALLICA

Metallica

METALLICA'S SELF-TITLED 1991 album was a top-to-bottom sonic overhaul. The band wanted to do something different. And did they ever. There were no thrash tempos, no abrupt time changes, and no angular riffs in 17/8 time. It had ballads. You could even hear the bass! From the band's perspective, it was a necessary change, but for the diehards, there was a feeling that the forces of commercialism had taken their band away. They did not care for this new, streamlined music one bit.

In truth, it's a good album if you listen to it for what it is and don't expect the ending of "Disposable Heroes" to suddenly materialize in the middle of "Nothing Else Matters." In fact, the couple of more up-tempo songs, like "Holier Than Thou" and "The Struggle Within," come off as Diet Thrash, phoned-in concessions to older fans who wanted to hear fast stuff. Those songs are merely faster than the slow stuff, so they don't even work as consolation prizes.

The best songs are the ones that demonstrate total commitment to the new agenda. They were looking to wipe the slate clean and start fresh, and the record is best served by the cuts that fall under that heading. "The God That Failed" and "My Friend of Misery" are rich and expansive, and "Sad But True" is heavy as hell, although according to *Metallica: The $24.95 Book* by Ben Apatoff, an early demo exists that's taken at an even slower tempo than what appears on the album. That doesn't appear to be in the *Metallica* thirtieth-anniversary box set, so if they wanted to throw it out there, at least one middle-aged author in Brooklyn would love to hear it.

The album topped the charts upon its release and is one of the highest-selling albums of all time, with twenty million copies certified sold in the United States alone as of 2025. That puts it in the same reaches of the charts as Michael Jackson's *Thriller*, Pink Floyd's *Dark Side of the Moon*, and Fleetwood Mac's *Rumours*. The commercial reaction to *Metallica* made them the biggest metal band in the world, a title they still hold.

Metallica signified a sea change, but not the one some people expected. Despite its success, it indicated that the thrash metal era was over. Its foremost purveyors had abandoned it. Megadeth, Slayer, and Anthrax would all release popular records in its wake, but the movement itself was beginning to subside, and in the new decade, it would become impossible to pretend otherwise.

FOR THE DIEHARDS, THERE WAS A FEELING THAT THE FORCES OF COMMERCIALISM HAD TAKEN THEIR BAND AWAY. THEY DID NOT CARE FOR THIS NEW, STREAMLINED MUSIC ONE BIT.

REVIEW

SLAYER

Decade of Aggression

DECADE OF AGGRESSION was Slayer's first legit live album, despite what the title of *Live Undead* would have you believe. It was released on October 22, 1991, almost exactly ten years to the day since Slayer's first gig at the Woodstock club on Halloween of 1981.

The performances are consistent throughout, so identifying the best songs is mainly a matter of identifying your favorite studio recordings. If you like the studio recording of "War Ensemble," you will like the version here, since it's really not any different.

If your tastes align more with the band's early era, there are performances from the Metal Blade era, and they benefit dramatically from the vastly improved production, which doesn't temper the primitive rage pervading those songs. In fact, the newfound clarity helps listeners pick out details that were hopelessly lost in a sea of reverb and financial limitations.

Despite being culled from three separate dates, it sounds like one concert, and if you saw the band during this era, it faithfully approximates what they were like at the time. True, no amount of state-of-the-art technology can capture the B.O. smells attendant at every Slayer concert. Neither can they capture the feeling of standing innocently in the crowd, minding your own business, and realizing that you're actually standing in the path of a wall of lunatics, seemingly in the throes of steroid rage, coming right at you. The only thing you might do to enhance the album is play aerial videos of Slayer mosh pits, which look like colonies of enraged carpenter ants, all trying to protect the queen.

Decade of Aggression consists uniformly of "warts and all" recordings with no overdubs. It's an unvarnished example of the band's frenzied performances, and every bit of the energy comes through. No recording will ever fully capture the full-spectrum insanity of a Slayer concert, but this album has as much as modern technology can capture.

THE ONLY THING YOU MIGHT DO TO ENHANCE THE ALBUM IS PLAY AERIAL VIDEOS OF SLAYER MOSH PITS, WHICH LOOK LIKE COLONIES OF ENRAGED CARPENTER ANTS, ALL TRYING TO PROTECT THE QUEEN.

Jeff Hanneman and Kerry King of Slayer in Denver on January 18, 1991, during the *Seasons in the Abyss* tour, which had Testament as the supporting act. Today, Testament and Exodus are the bands most frequently cited by Big Four band members as groups they would allow into an expanded Big Six.

CHAPTER 12

1992: INTO THE LUNGS OF HELL

1981	1982	1983	1984	1985	1986

LEFT: James Hetfield rubs aloe on burns sustained when he accidentally wandered into the path of onstage pyrotechnics. OPPOSITE: Dave Mustaine of Megadeth at London's Hammersmith Odeon on September 30, 1992. The band was selling records and playing to large audiences, but soon they would become *persona non grata* to the greater music business.

It may not have been immediately apparent, but in 1992, popular culture was changing. Things were a certain way when Metallica had entered the studio in 1990 to start work on their next record. They were very different now.

"When we were making *Metallica*, nobody even knew who the fuck Kurt Cobain was," Hammett told *Louder* in 2022. By August 1992, there was no one alive who didn't know who he was.

The fortunes of the thrash metal bands didn't instantly deflate on January 1, 1992. Megadeth released their next album with the *Rust in Peace* lineup, *Countdown to Extinction*, that July, and it fell just one spot short of the top, held back from the pinnacle by Billy Ray Cyrus's *Some Gave All*, which featured the crime against humanity known as "Achy Breaky Heart."

Metal was still big business, as evidenced by a joint Metallica and Guns N' Roses tour. On August 8, 1992, Hetfield suffered third-degree burns during a performance of "Fade to Black" when he accidentally walked into the wrong spot onstage and found himself on the business end of the pyrotechnics. They finished the tour with Hetfield on vocals while John Marshall of Metal Church filled in for him on guitar, just as he had done in 1986 when Hetfield broke his arm skateboarding.

That was just how Metallica functioned. There was no bereavement leave and no sick days, even for third-degree burns.

Anthrax started 1992 strong. After touring Europe with Public Enemy, the band was courted by Elektra Records, which signed them to a $4 million deal. At the same time, Joey Belladonna was fired, which Ian recalled was a heartbreaking surprise the singer hadn't seen coming. The only upside was that Anthrax had done the right thing and given him an equal share of the Elektra advance.

He was replaced by former Armored Saint vocalist John Bush, and Anthrax released *Sound of White Noise* in 1993. It reached #7 on the *Billboard* chart, their highest placement ever, but they lost some fans when they changed the singer. (Bands can change a bassist without fans noticing or caring, but a singer can be a bridge too far.) "We understood that we had crossed some of our fans," Ian said.

The real problems set in as Anthrax worked on its next record, 1995's *Stomp 442*. The band had also parted ways with lead guitarist Dan Spitz, but that wasn't the issue. There had been a change of guard at Elektra, and the team that had signed them was a casualty of the corporate reorganization.

The new CEO met with band manager Steve Barnett and told him she never would have signed Anthrax to the label to begin with. Elektra was contractually obligated to release *Stomp 442*, but its efforts ended there. They just released it into the void with no promotion, and it starved to death.

By this time, metal was less popular than before, but it wasn't dead. There were still fans out there. It was the record companies killing it, and while Anthrax never lost their hardcore fans, audiences began to shrink.

"We played venues one-third the size of the places we were booked at in '93 and '94," Ian said. "We went from being a band that went gold with every record since 1987 to a group that could barely sell one hundred thousand records on a major label."

They still had one album left in their Elektra deal. The label didn't want it, so they paid the band the rest of what they were contractually owed and cut them loose. Prospective labels only cared about how their last album had sold, and since it had been buried by the label, the answer was "not much." Anthrax had released a string of gold albums, but that didn't matter to the labels. "We were only as good as our last album," Ian recalled.

Things became more difficult for Megadeth as well. They had been signed by a team that understood nurturing a band's career, but that team was gone in the same type of corporate reorganization that had affected Elektra. It was something the entire music industry was going through at the time.

"Every time a new Capitol president came in, it was like your mom getting remarried, and you are the redheaded stepchild," Mustaine told *Metal Hammer* in 2019.

He took responsibility for some of the band's 1990s misfortunes. In 1993, Megadeth embarked on a tour with Aerosmith, the band whose singer, Steven Tyler, had called Ellefson to check on him a few years earlier. Mustaine said that Megadeth received somewhat shabby treatment and didn't get a satisfactory sound check or a long enough time to play, so when a radio DJ asked why the sets were so short, he responded in his inimitable way: "We don't have a long time to play because Aerosmith don't have a long time to live."

LEFT: Scott Ian of Anthrax at a benefit concert for LifeBeat in Hollywood, California, on March 12, 1995. The guy behind him is an unidentified camera operator not affiliated with Anthrax in any way, shape, or form, so don't look at him. OPPOSITE: Joey Belladonna of Anthrax and Flavor Flav of Public Enemy in the Netherlands on January 18, 1992. The fusion of rap and metal may seem like no big deal today, but at the time, it was groundbreaking.

Megadeth were kicked off the tour, which they found out at a restaurant. The waitress asked what the band was doing in town, and when they said they were playing that night with Aerosmith, she said she had heard on the radio that Jackyl was opening.

Slayer had a slightly easier time of it than Anthrax and Megadeth, in part because they had never been in the Top 10 or made particularly commercial music—there was no high perch to fall from. Still, they noticed what was going on around them.

Reign in Blood seemed like the absolute fastest, heaviest, and most extreme metal album possible upon its 1986 release. Almost anyone who listened to the final section of "Raining Blood" for the first time came to that conclusion, and it was widely believed that its speed and aggression could never be topped. That conclusion quickly turned into a dare for the next wave of underground metal musicians, and many bands formed with the sole intention of beating that one record.

Kreator front man Mille Petrozza told *Metal Hammer* in 2019 that the situation led to an influx of derivative bands that sent demo tapes to whoever was looking to sign the next Metallica. The scene quickly became oversaturated. "There were so many shitty thrash bands jumping on the bandwagon."

It was tempting to blame grunge and alternative rock, but the truth is that there had been too much thrash metal, too fast, and it quickly went stale, exactly what would happen to grunge a few years later. The reality is that the bands that had formed to hop on a trend fell victim to their own life expectancies, while those who had formed thrash metal bands because they loved the

TAMA.
TAMA

ABOVE: Jeff Hanneman and Kerry King of Slayer at Roseland in New York City. King is to be commended for embracing male pattern baldness and just shaving his head. OPPOSITE: Megadeth in Turin, Italy, on June 22, 1993. David Ellefson, Dave Mustaine, and Marty Friedman (*foreground, from left*) enjoy the experience of having drummer Nick Menza tower over them.

music pressed on. "Lots of bands split up," Petrozza said. "But some bands kept fighting."

Slayer was one of the bands that kept fighting, although they wisely stuck to their own established sound and didn't try to compete with the new guys. Death metal and grindcore had already outpaced *Reign in Blood*, and they got topped in terms of evil imagery, too. Look no further than Norway's Mayhem, whose bassist Varg Vikernes burned down centuries-old churches to protest Christianity, then murdered a bandmate.

The genre seemed most moribund on June 4, 1996, when Metallica released *Load*. There was no thrash metal on it anywhere, an offense they compounded by headlining the alternative rock festival Lollapalooza. However, both of those transgressions pale in comparison to their worst one: They cut their hair. Nothing signaled that this wasn't your father's Metallica quite like that.

Despite this offense, Metallica remained popular as ever. In fact, in 1999, *Metallica* won the Diamond Award from the RIAA for selling more than ten million copies. The following year, Ulrich testified before the United States Senate about the file-sharing platform Napster, which allowed users to illegally download music for free. When he testified, many cried foul. How could he ruin everybody's good time?

In 2024, Charlie Benante told the *Irish Times* that Ulrich and Metallica were correct in sounding the alarm. They took a lot of grief for speaking out, but today it's clear that every creative person on earth owes them a debt of gratitude for trying to

The tragic events of 9/20. Metallica (from left: Jason Newsted, Kirk Hammett, and Lars Ulrich) in Milan on September 20, 1996, after committing the unforgivable sin of cutting their hair. Eight years later, they gave us the documentary *Some Kind of Monster*, which offered viewers an up-close-and-personal look at a band on the verge of unraveling.

ensure artists were paid for their work. "They were protecting *their* art . . . so that some asshole does not come along and take *your* art," Benante explained.

In 2001, Jason Newsted left the band, citing health considerations. Many suspected the real reason dated back to his treatment when he joined. "I think the general feeling in the band is that he was never treated with the respect that he deserved," producer Flemming Rasmussen told *Metal Hammer* in 2016.

Perhaps even more telling was something journalist Bob Mack said in his 1991 *SPIN* feature on the band, the one in which he insisted Metallica were never very good. He may not have cared for their music, but he said something that couldn't be dismissed: "Although he's been in the band over five years, he still isn't the bassist," Mack wrote. "That title will always belong to the late Cliff Burton, who was crushed when the group's tour bus rolled over in Sweden on September 27, 1986."

Newsted never brought anything less than 100 percent to the gig, something his former bandmates make a point of mentioning whenever they can. That was never the issue. The issue was that the bus accident was a wound that had never closed despite the band's efforts to soldier on. Maybe it was because they insisted on soldiering on. Whatever the case, when Newsted left, the issue remained unprocessed and as potent as ever.

The 2004 documentary *Some Kind of Monster* shows the band finally confronting the emotional reality. It was supposed to document the making of a new album, but when Hetfield entered rehab in 2001, the band began to unravel. Ulrich told *Loud and Quiet*'s Daniel Dylan Wray in 2018 that it was the only time he thought the band might break up. "For about six months, it was a little uncertain," he said.

The documentary featured Mustaine in a pivotal sequence. He had suffered radial neuropathy, which made him unable to play guitar, and his appearance coincided with his ultimately temporary retirement from Megadeth. He said Ulrich had invited him to the band's group therapy session but didn't tell him it was being filmed until he arrived, which he characterized in his memoir as an "ambush." He went ahead and opened up to Ulrich anyway, saying he regretted the behavior that led to his firing.

Despite objecting to the footage being included in the movie, it ended up in it anyway. The sequence is poignant and shows a side of Mustaine that does him and his emotional honesty a lot of credit. He comes off very well and watching him unburden himself of issues he had carried for decades is something you wish he had done sooner.

Metallica was inducted into the Rock & Roll Hall of Fame in 2009. Rob Trujillo had since become the band's bassist, a position he still holds as of 2026. All four bands were still together, which defied a lot of expectations, considering the downturn in popularity that all things thrash metal had weathered.

Ulrich asked Ian and Benante to come to the induction ceremony, and when they did, he asked what they thought of all four bands playing together. It wasn't an offer they really needed to think about. "I remember saying to Scott, 'We've got to get our shit together and do this,'" Benante told the *Aquarian* in 2017.

By "get our shit together," he meant "get a singer." Anthrax had tracked a new album, but getting someone to sing on it was a problem. Bush, who had joined for *Sound of White Noise*, was now a family man and didn't want to be away from them on the extensive tour that a new album would necessitate. That cleared the way for the band to reunite the lineup that birthed *Among the Living*, or at least 80 percent of it, since Dan Spitz wasn't involved. Would Belladonna be up for it despite his unexpected 1992 dismissal?

"All I ever wanted to do was be in the band," he said. "Let's do it again."

Around that time, Ellefson's phone rang, and it was Mustaine. The two had experienced an acrimonious falling-out after Mustaine's first attempt at retirement, due to money and business matters that went awry. After extensive physical therapy, the guitarist regained the ability to play guitar and Megadeth returned, but without its original bassist. The falling-out had been an ugly one, with lawyers and large sums of money involved, and when Mustaine returned to active duty in 2004, it remained unresolved.

Metallica at the Rock and Roll Hall of Fame Induction Ceremony in Cleveland, Ohio, on April 4, 2009. Jason Newsted (*far left*) had left the band in 2001, and Robert Trujillo (*second from left*) became the next new guy. He's still with the band decades later.

David Ellefson and Dave Mustaine of Megadeth perform during the Stone Free Festival at London's O2 Arena on June 16, 2018. Ellefson had been out of the band since 2002 and rejoined for the Big Four concerts, staying until 2021.

Mustaine said the Big Four dates were coming together and Megadeth would be involved. Would Ellefson do it? A lot of unpleasantness had gone down over the past few years, and even though the idea was very appealing to him, he still had misgivings. He said it was a discussion with his wife, Julie, that really convinced him to participate. "You haven't been really happy since you left the band," she told him. "Do it because you're his friend."

Slayer had also been through a lot before accepting their invitation to perform. They parted ways with Lombardo in 1992 and replaced him with Forbidden drummer Paul Bostaph, who was there when the band released *God Hates Us All* on September 11, 2001, which could really only happen to Slayer. Unfortunately, he was sidelined by an elbow injury in the middle of the European tour, so they reached out to Lombardo, who finished the tour and then stayed in the band.

Everyone had agreed to be involved. Despite the divergent paths they had all taken to get there, all four bands were strangely in the same place when the shows were booked, and it wasn't just an opportunity for the bands to tour together. It was a moment for all of them to celebrate their survival, as bands and as a genre.

The first date was June 16, 2010, in Warsaw, and the June 22 date at the Sonisphere Festival in Sofia, Bulgaria, was filmed for a live broadcast and later released on home video. It was released in November as *The Big Four: Live from Sofia, Bulgaria*. On April 23, 2011, the bands appeared in Indio, California.

While he had performed on the European dates, Hanneman was unable to do the 2011 dates. He had contracted the flesh-eating bacterial condition necrotic fasciitis, which was debilitating to his right arm and made him unable to play guitar. Gary Holt of Exodus stepped up to play in his place, and Araya said he fit right in.

"Gary Holt is a really great guitar player, and he's a really good friend," Araya told the Brazilian podcast *Wikimetal*. He was also on the 1985 *North American Combat* tour when Araya made number one in Cronos's hair, a pivotal moment in Slayer history.

Hanneman made a surprise appearance at the end of Slayer's Indio set to play "South of Heaven" and "Angel of Death." He hoped it meant he would make a full recovery and come back soon.

Tom Araya and Kerry King of Slayer on November 14, 2019, in Moline, Illinois, during the band's farewell tour. Although you can't see him in this photo, the drums are helmed by former Forbidden drummer Paul Bostaph, the man who first heard *Reign in Blood* at a 1986 house party and concluded, "We're fucked."

"It was so fucking great playing again," he told *Rolling Stone* in 2011. "It was rough for me to sit on the bench, watching the guys."

After the end of Metallica's set, almost every member of the Big Four bands in attendance assembled onstage together to play Diamond Head's "Am I Evil?" The sight of Mustaine playing it with his old band again was quite simply something no one ever thought they would see. They were more likely to encounter Bigfoot.

After five July dates in Europe, the bands went to New York City's Yankee Stadium on September 14, 2011. It was one day after the release of Anthrax's new album, *Worship Music*, which debuted at #12 on the *Billboard* chart. It was a moment that would have been impossible to fathom during the late 1990s, when they were on the outs with the music business. "It was like we were toxic to the touch," Ian said. "Like real anthrax."

What a difference a decade makes. One hopes the Elektra CEO who had dropped them was aware Anthrax was doing just fine without them. Perhaps more than any of the other Big Four bands, Anthrax had been treated the shittiest by the music industry, which made the September 14, 2011, gig all the sweeter. "The Big Four show at Yankee Stadium was the greatest moment in my life as a musician, hands down," Ian said.

Anthrax had survived by sticking to their guns and staying true to their vision. They hung on as the business became increasingly corporate, and even when the bottom fell out in the streaming age. By not breaking up, they had proven more durable than the music industry that had rejected them.

"Maybe we stayed around so long we outlasted all the bullshit," Ian said.

As of this writing, all four bands are either still active or sort of active. Neither Anthrax nor Metallica ever broke up or announced retirement. Slayer played their final show on November 30, 2019, only to reunite for festival shows in 2024, and announce concerts for late 2026 to commemorate the 40th anniversary of *Reign in Blood*.

In 2025, Megadeth announced the release of their final album and farewell tour. Mustaine was suffering from arthritis and Dupuytren contracture, a hand condition that made playing guitar very difficult. However, he told *Kerrang!* the farewell tour could last "three to five years," and if that outside estimate comes to fruition, he will be seventy years old when it winds down in 2031. That sure doesn't sound like someone who's quitting.

This is all to say that while the thrash metal era is over, the music is still very much alive. The Big Four has seen to it. They and their genre might have been pronounced dead, but they're still making a lot of noise.

In other words, rumors of the Big Four's demise have been greatly exaggerated. Long may they reign.

Dave Mustaine of Megadeth at London's O2 Arena on October 26, 2025. He had already announced his intention to retire, but we'll believe he's retired when we see him in Boca Raton golfing with Alice Cooper.

SOURCES

BOOKS

Ellefson, David, and Joel McIver. *My Life with Deth: Discovering Meaning in a Life of Rock & Roll*. Howard Books, 2013.

Ian, Scott, and Jon Wiederhorn. *I'm the Man: The Story of That Guy from Anthrax*. Da Capo Press, 2014.

Layden, Joe, and Dave Mustaine. *Mustaine: A Heavy Metal Memoir*. Dey Street Books, 2011.

ARTICLES

Alago, Michael. "The Inside Story of the Show That Scored Metallica a Major Label Deal." *Classic Rock*, September 20, 2022.

Alderslade, Merlin. "'We Knew We Were Good, and You Could Feel It When We Got Onstage.' Dave Lombardo Remembers Slayer's First Ever Show—and the Craziest Thing He's Ever Seen at a Gig." *Metal Hammer*, October 27, 2023.

Armstrong, Chuck. "Jason Newsted Reflects on 25th Anniversary of Metallica's . . . *And Justice For All*." *Loudwire*, August 24, 2013.

Armstrong, Chuck. "Metallica's 1985 Tour Took Them to Kansas City for the First Time Ever." *Ultimate Metallica*, February 16, 2023.

Armstrong, Chuck. "Ron McGovney—Biography." *Ultimate Metallica*, October 8, 2011.

Barrios, Joel. "Tom G. Warrior Talks Tape Trading and the Lack of Mystique in Modern Metal: 'You Had to Really Put an Effort into Discovering Music.'" *Metal Injection*, August 18, 2023.

Bennett, J. "Slayer." *Decibel*, August 2006.

Bienstock, Richard. "I Went to Lars's House, and He Played Me the Tape of 'Hit the Lights.' I Said, 'This Song Sucks. You Need More Guitar Solos.'" *Guitar World*, December 12, 2024.

Blistein, Jon. "MTV's Music-Only Channels Are Officially Going Dark." *Rolling Stone*, December 31, 2025.

Brannigan, Paul. "James Hetfield and Lars Ulrich Were Confused, Angry, and 'Freaked Out' When They First Saw Metallica's 'One' Video." *Metal Hammer*, September 20, 2022.

Cecolini, Vinny. "Charlie Benante Discusses the Highs and Lows of One of Metal's Big Four." *JAM*, March 2013.

Chantler, Chris. "How the 1990s Almost Killed Thrash Metal." *Metal Hammer*, September 20, 2022.

Cherry Bomb. "Sad But True: The Robbery in Boston That Inspired Metallica's 'Fade to Black.'" *Metal Injection*, October 6, 2020.

Childers, Chad. "Biggest Selling Metal Album of All Time Reaches Rare Milestone." *Loudwire*, May 28, 2025.

"Chris Poland Reflects on Long-Term Impact of Mustaine's Accusations: 'It Finally Dawned on Me Just How Much Damage That Really Did.'" *Sonic Perspectives*, May 19, 2025.

Coffman, Tim. "The Song That Got Kirk Hammett the Gig in Metallica: 'We Instantly Knew It Was the Right Thing.'" *Far Out*, May 11, 2024.

Daly, Joe. "'The Blueprint for the Beginning of Death Metal.' How Slayer Dragged Metal to New Depths of Evil with *Show No Mercy*." *Metal Hammer*, December 6, 2023.

Daly, Joe. "Every Anthrax Album Ranked from Worst to Best." *Metal Hammer*, January 23, 2024.

"Dave Mustaine: 'I Would Have Kicked Me Out of Metallica.'" *Metal Hammer*, September 20, 2022.

"Dave Mustaine On Metallica: 'I Wrote a Lot of Their Music That Made Them.'" *Blabbermouth*, May 28, 2025.

"David Ellefson: How Alice in Chains Ended Up Opening for Megadeth, Slayer, and Anthrax." *Blabbermouth*, July 22, 2020.

Diehl, Matt. "The Big 4 Put Aside Their Differences for Spectacular Metal Show." *Rolling Stone*, April 25, 2011.

DiVita, Joe. "Lars Ulrich Reveals Who Came Up with the Name 'Metallica' (It Wasn't Anyone in the Band)." *Loudwire*, September 26, 2023.

Doe, Bernard. "Anthrax—Anarchy in the USA." *Metal Forces*, Issue 10 (1985).

Doe, Bernard. "Anthrax/Onslaught Live Review." *Metal Forces*, Issue 18 (1986).

Doe, Bernard. "Anthrax *State of Euphoria* Review." *Metal Forces*, Issue 31 (1988).

Doe, Bernard. "Megadeth—Love It to Death." *Metal Forces*, Issue 12 (1985).

Doe, Bernard. "Metallica—Bang 'Em Hard." *Metal Forces*, Issue 3 (1984).

Doe, Bernard. "Metallica—Killing Time Again." *Metal Forces*, June 2016.

Doe, Bernard. "Metallica—Lightning Raiders." *Metal Forces*, Issue 8 (1984).

Doe, Bernard. "Slayer Demo Review." *Metal Forces*, Issue 2 (1983).

Doe, Bernard. "Slayer—Let It Bleed." *Metal Forces*, Issue 20 (1986).

Doe, Bernard. "Slayer *Show No Mercy* Review." *Metal Forces*, Issue 3 (1984).

Doe, Bernard. "Slayer—Total Devotion." *Metal Forces*, Issue 66 (1991).

Doe, Bernard. "Stormtroopers of Death—Deadly Nightmare." *Metal Forces*, Issue 15 (1985).

Doughton, K. J. "Slayer—Killer Instinct." *Metal Forces*, Issue 6 (1984).

Eglinton, Mark. "Th1rt3en Best: Dave Mustaine of Megadeth's Favourite Albums." *Quietus*, March 16, 2016.

Elliott, Paul. "The Big Interview: Dave Mustaine." *Classic Rock*, September 20, 2022.

Elliott, Paul. "'I've Seen a Lot of Things. Supernatural Things. I've Seen the Place Between Heaven and Hell': The Outrageous Life of King Diamond, the Occult Metal Icon Metallica Love and Gene Simmons Wanted to Sue." *Metal Hammer*, October 6, 2024.

Enis, Eli. "Dave Lombardo: My Life Story." *Revolver*, May 26, 2023.

Everley, Dave. "Kirk Hammett: 'I Was Sitting on the Toilet When I Got the Call to Join Metallica.'" *Metal Hammer*, September 20, 2022.

Everley, Dave. "'Metallica and Slayer Were Never Close': An Interview with the Man Who Discovered Metallica." *Metal Hammer*, September 20, 2022.

Everley, Dave. "Slayer's *Reign in Blood*: The Epic Oral History of Thrash's Greatest Album." *Metal Hammer*, October 7, 2021.

Everley, Dave. "We Were Like, 'These Guys Are Just Like Us, This Is Crazy! We Want to Hack Things Up with Machetes with Them!'" *Metal Hammer*, May 10, 2024.

"The First Time I Saw Slayer: Scott Ian." *Kerrang!*, June 27, 2018.

"Former Megadeth Drummer Chuck Behler Comments on Jeff Young's Remarks Towards Dave Mustaine—I Really Don't Think People Are Too Interested in Hearing About the Petty Little Things That Happened Between Us Back Then." *Brave Words*, December 28, 2009.

Fricke, David. "Don't Tread on Me: Metallica's James Hetfield." *Rolling Stone*, April 15, 1993.

Fricke, David. "Metallica: From Metal to Main Street." *Rolling Stone*, November 14, 1991.

Fricke, David. "Metallica: Heavy Metal Justice." *Rolling Stone*, January 12, 1989.

Garza, Janiss. "Slayer Orchestrates Fearsome Intensity." *Los Angeles Times*, August 15, 1988.

Gehlke, David. "Slayer—'The Cushion Riot Concert' Exclusive Excerpt from *Slayer 66 2/3: The Jeff & Dave Years*." *Dead Rhetoric*, January 11, 2014.

Genzlinger, Neil. "Jon Zazula, Early Promoter of Heavy Metal, Dies at 69." *New York Times*, February 9, 2022.

Genzlinger, Neil. "Marsha Zazula, 'Metal Matriarch' of Metallica and Others, Dies at 68." *New York Times*, January 16, 2021.

Grow, Kory. "Megadeth's Dave Mustaine: My Life in 15 Songs." *Rolling Stone*, January 11, 2017.

Grow, Kory. "Metallica's Lars Ulrich on Lemmy: 'His Spirit Will Always Live in Us.'" *Rolling Stone*, December 29, 2015.

Grow, Kory. "Metallica's Lars Ulrich Recalls 'F—ed Up' 1989 Grammy Loss." *Rolling Stone*, January 27, 2014.

Grow, Kory. "Slayer's Kerry King: My 10 Favorite Metal Albums." *Rolling Stone*, July 14, 2017.

Grow, Kory. "Slayer's Kerry King on Why Judas Priest Matter." *Rolling Stone*, March 10, 2022.

"Guitarist Lloyd Grant: How I Ended Up Playing on Original Recording of Metallica's 'Hit the Lights.'" *Blabbermouth*, March 28, 2015.

Hart, Ron. "Anthrax's Charlie Benante Reflects on Polarizing *State of Euphoria* for Its 30th Anniversary Reissue." *Billboard*, September 19, 2018.

Hickie, James. "Megadeth: 'The Body Will Disappear, But the Legend Will Remain. And the Music Will Go on Forever.'" *Kerrang!*, November 12, 2025.

Hill, Stephen. "Jason Newsted on Joining Metallica: 'Cliff Burton's Mom Told Me, "You're the One."'" *Metal Hammer*, September 20, 2022.

Hobson, Rich. "'I Thought They Were Taking the Piss': Ozzy Osbourne on His First Meeting with Metallica." *Metal Hammer*, September 20, 2022.

Huey, Steve. "*State of Euphoria* Review." *AllMusic*.

"Interview with Ex-Megadeth Guitarist Jeff Young." *Metal Underground*, December 29, 2009.

"Jason Newsted Speaks on How Other Musicians Treated Him When He Joined Metallica, Reveals What He Thought of Pantera at Moscow Show." *Ultimate Guitar*, September 9, 2021.

"Joey Belladonna Had 'No Clue' Who Anthrax Were When He Auditioned for Them." *Metal Hammer*, May 11, 2021.

Junior, Chris. "Jethro Tull's Ian Anderson Thought Metallica Would Win First-Ever Hard Rock/Metal Grammy." *Ultimate Classic Rock*, February 12, 2012.

Kennelty, Greg. "Metallica's Lars Ulrich Cites Iron Maiden as Band's Biggest Influence." *Metal Injection*, September 5, 2020.

Konow, David. "Exploring the Roots of the Mid-80s Metal/Punk Crossover with Kerry King, Scott Ian, and Gary Holt." *Vice*, October 9, 2015.

Krgin, Borivoj. "Slayer—a Man for All Seasons." *Metal Forces*, Issue 60 (1991).

Krovatin, Chris. "The Man Who Discovered Metallica Remembers Thrash Metal's Ragtag Salad Days." *Kerrang!*, October 10, 2019.

"Lars Ulrich Looks Back on *Kill 'Em All*—One Band You Can't Leave Out of a Conversation About Metallica's Influences Are Mercyful Fate." *Brave Words*, March 3, 2019.

"Lars Ulrich Reflects on Metallica's First Ever Gig." *Kerrang!*, March 19, 2019.

Larson, Bob. "Desperately Seeking Satan." *SPIN*, May 1989.

Louie, Tim. "Worship Anthrax: An Interview with Charlie Benante." *Aquarian*, May 27, 2015.

Machado, Nando. "Interview with Tom Araya (Slayer)." *Wikimetal*, June 2, 2011.

Mack, Bob. "Precious Metal." *SPIN*, October 1991.

Mackay, Emily. "Metallica's Lars Ulrich: Maybe We'll Do Our Rendition of 'Wonderwall.'" *Guardian*, May 31, 2014.

Massie, Andrew. "Interview: Charlie Benante—Anthrax." *The Rockpit*, November 6, 2018.

McGreevy, Ronan. "Anthrax's Charlie Benante: 'I Was Always a Big U2 Fan. They Just Got Better and Better.'" *Irish Times*, November 23, 2024.

McIver, Joel. "The 1000 Days That Changed Metallica." *Louder*, September 20, 2022.

McQueen, Gregg. "Box Sets, Beer, and Black Math: An Interview with Anthrax Drummer Charlie Benante." *Aquarian*, March 29, 2017.

"Megadeth's David Ellefson: How I Became One of the 1st Metal Bassists to Use 5-String Bass." *Ultimate Guitar*, January 11, 2019.

"Metallica's Black Sabbath Induction Speech Available." *Blabbermouth*, March 15, 2006.

Mills, Matt. "They Politely Said, 'We Will Never Air This. You Are Banned from MTV.' Scott Ian Reveals Which Song Got Anthrax Banned in the 80s." *Metal Hammer*, December 27, 2024.

"My KSDT Interview with Frank Bello from Anthrax, April 1, 1988." *Takin' A Ride*, January 14, 2025.

Neely, Kim. "Slayer *South of Heaven*." *Rolling Stone*, October 6, 1988.

Nichols, Vlad. "Original Anthrax Bassist & Cofounder Speaks on Being 'Thrown Out' of the Band: 'I Had No Choice.'" *Ultimate Guitar*, January 5, 2024.

Oberkrieser, Brandon. "Metallica and the Historical Relevance of Their 1985 Day on the Green Performance." *MetalTalk*, May 29, 2020.

O'Neill, Christina. "Metallica Producer: . . . *And Justice for All* Bassist Was Brilliant." *Metal Hammer*, March 18, 2016.

O'Neill, Eamon. "Anthrax Charlie Benante *eonmusic* Interview." *eonmusic*, April 2021.

Pareles, Jon. "For Slayer, the Mania Is the Message." *New York Times*, September 3, 1988.

Perlah, Jeff. "Metallica's James Hetfield Rides the Lightning with *Newsweek*." *Newsweek*, February 9, 2017.

Polcaro, Rafael. "Lars Ulrich Tells How They Chose the Name Metallica for the Band." *Rock and Roll Garage*, January 5, 2018.

Rivadavia, Eduardo. "When Metallica's James Hetfield and Lars Ulrich Met." *Ultimate Classic Rock*, May 2, 2016.

Roberts, Rachel. "Dave Mustaine Discusses How Diamond Head Were Early Influence on Metallica." *Guitar*, January 10, 2023.

Rosenberg, Axl. "Metal Blade Founder/CEO Brian Slagel: The *MetalSucks* Interview." *MetalSucks*, November 19, 2012.

Ruskell, Nick. "The 25 Greatest Thrash Metal Albums Ever." *Kerrang!*, October 26, 2020.

Samuels, David. "Q&A: Scott Ian." *Tablet*, September 13, 2011.

"Slayer: Unpublished 1983 Interview with Kerry King and Jeff Hanneman Now Available." *Blabbermouth*, March 29, 2012.

"Slayer's Kerry King: 'Religion Is the Funnest Thing to Make Fun Of.'" *Metal Hammer*, November 8, 2016.

Sword, Harry. "Raining Mud: Tom Araya of Slayer Interviewed." *Quietus*, September 22, 2015.

Wall, Mick. "*The $5.98 EP*: How *Garage Days* Pulled Metallica Back from the Brink." *Classic Rock*, September 20 2022.

Wardlaw, Matt. "How Metallica Changed the World with Their Most Polarizing Album." *Ultimate Classic Rock*, August 10, 2021.

Wiederhorn, Jon. "Clash of the Titans Tour: Iron Giants." *Guitar World*, April 13, 2010.

"When Lou Reed Heard the Ramones for the First Time." *Riot Fest*, November 15, 2017.

"Where to Start with . . . Megadeth." *Kerrang!*, May 1, 2009.

Winwood, Ian. "Slayer: The Stories Behind 20 of Their Biggest Songs." *Kerrang!*, June 16, 2021.

Wray, Daniel Dylan. "Lars Ulrich Recounts How Metallica Regrouped in 1987 After the Death of Their Friend and Bassist." *Loud and Quiet*, May 14, 2018.

"10 songs That Invented Thrash Metal, According to Anthrax Guitarist Scott Ian." *Classic Rock*, January 20, 2024.

"The 100 Greatest Singers: Inside the Ballots." *Rolling Stone*, November 12, 2008.

"200 Greatest Metal Guitar Solos." August 5, 2008.

WEBSITES

anthrax.com

black-sabbath.com

deathridersblog.wordpress.com

espguitars.com

megadeth.com

metalblade.com

metalforcesmagazine.com

metallica.com

metalupdate.com

slayer.net

theconcertdatabase.com

twinpeaksarchive.blogspot.com

ultimatemetal.com

IMAGE CREDITS

B = bottom, L = left, R = right, T = top

Alamy: 15 (Morten Kjaer/Gonzales Photo), 17L (Madi), 18L (Ulf Palm/TT News Agency), 24 (Pictorial Press), 36 (Robert Hoetink), 54 (Robert Hoetink), 55T (Robert Hoetink), 74 (John Atashian), 85 (Anders Andersson/TT News Agency), 88T (© Christopher Helton via ZUMA Press Wire), 90T (Jeff Smith), 91 (Jeff Smith), 116 (© Kevin Estrada/Media Punch), 118L (John Atashian), 118R (John Atashian), 118 (dpa picture alliance), 121T (dpa picture alliance), 130 (Uli Nusko), 133T (© Kevin Estrada/MediaPunch), 138 (© Kevin Estrada/ MediaPunch), 152 (Pat Johnson/MediaPunch), 165 (© Kevin Estrada/MediaPunch), 167 (Barry King), 176 (Fabio Diena), 178T (Fabio Diena), 178B (Maximum Film), 179L (Fabio Diena), 180 (© Daniel DeSlover/ZUMA Wire), 181 (Sipa USA/Alamy Live News). **Wayne Archibald:** 8, 30, 37T, 40, 50, 58B. **Avalon:** 42 (Pete Cronin), 115 (John Atashian). **Henri Clauser/FastImage via Frank White Photo Agency:** 60. **Getty Images:** 7 (*Metal Hammer*), 10 (Roberta Bayley/Redferns), 11T (Images), 11B (Robert Ellis/Hulton Archive), 14 (Michael Ochs Archives), 16 (Gus Stewart/Redferns), 17R (Fin Costello/Redferns), 19T (Joel Slevin/ Michael Ochs Archives), 19B (Fin Costello/Redferns), 27B (Oli Scarff/AFP), 28 (C Brandon/ Redferns), 32 (Fryderyk Gabowicz/picture alliance), 51 (Pete Cronin/Redferns), 61 (Pete Cronin/Redferns), 66 (Niels van Iperen/Hulton Archive), 71 (Icon and Image/Michael Ochs Archives), 73 (Fin Costello/Redferns), 80 (Koh Hasebe/Shinko Music/Hulton Archive), 82R (Icon and Image/Michael Ochs Archives), 87 (Chris Walter/WireImage), 96 (Paul Natkin), 98 (Icon and Image/Michael Ochs Archives), 99L (Niels van Iperen/Hulton Archive), 100T (Paul Natkin), 100B (Jim Steinfeldt/Michael Ochs Archives), 101 (Mike Cameron/Redferns), 102 (Brian Rasic/Hulton Archive), 103T (Larry Hulst/Hulton Archive), 104R (Jim Steinfeldt/ Michael Ochs Archives), 105 (Paul Natkin), 106 (Paul Natkin/WireImage), 108 (Mike Cameron/Redferns), 118 (Paul Bergen/Redferns), 120 (Michael Ochs Archives), 122–123 (Mirrorpix), 131 (Pete Still/Redferns), 132 (Jeff Smith), 134 (Niels van Iperen/Hulton Archive), 135 (Hulton Archive), 139 (Paul Natkin/WireImage), 141 (Jeff Kravitz/FilmMagic), 144 (Mick Hutson/Redferns), 147 (Lisa Haun/Michael Ochs Archives), 148 (Mick Hutson/ Redferns), 149 (Mick Hutson/Redferns), 150 (Goedefroit Music/Hulton Archive), 158 (Al Seib/*Los Angeles Times*), 162 (Lisa Lake/Michael Ochs Archives), 163 (Raymond Boyd/ Michael Ochs Archives), 164 (Mick Hutson/Redferns), 166 (Ann Summa/Hulton Archive), 172 (Ian Dickson/Redferns), 173R (John Storey/The Chronicle Collection), 174 (Niels van Iperen/Hulton Archive), 175L (Steve Eichner), 177 (Patti Ouderkirk/WireImage), 179R (Chiaki Nozu/WireImage). **Kevin Hodapp via Frank White Photo Agency:** 26, 44, 48, 55B, 56, 57T, 57B, 72B. **Lowell Katz:** 23, 37B, 38, 43T, 45, 52L, 52R, 58T, 75R. **Krasner/Trebitz via Frank White Photo Agency:** 26, 137B, 142, 145. **Alex Mitram/FastImage via Frank White Photo Agency:** 70. **Courtesy Bill O'Leary:** 160, 170. **Press Image:** 88B. **Pat Prince via Frank White Photo Agency:** 68. **Frank White via Frank White Photo Agency:** 2, 20, 22, 25T, 27T, 29, 34, 39, 59, 69, 72T, 83, 84, 86, 89, 92, 112, 128, 136, 137T, 156, 159, 161.

ACKNOWLEDGMENTS

First and foremost, thank you to Dennis Pernu of Quarto/ Motorbooks for letting me write this book. I never stopped badgering you about when we could do it already, so I hope the outcome was worth putting up with my perpetual whining. As I said in the acknowledgments to *Iron Maiden at 50*, long may we reign.

Thank you to my parents, Albert and Joanna Bukszpan; my sister, Claudia Rutherford; and my mother-in-law, Valborg Linn, for supporting me in every way throughout my career. Writing for a living has its ups and downs, but you have all been there for me as I grind away at it. None of this would have happened without you.

Thank you to my son, Roman, for keeping me going through the hard times by singing Megadeth's "Symphony of Destruction" in a Louis Armstrong voice. That was "baller," to borrow a phrase from you youngs. Thank you to my wife, Asia, for whom I played Anthrax's *Among the Living* in my initial adolescent attempt to woo her. You are the love of my life and having you with me in my "veteran rock journalist" years has meant everything to me. I love you and Roman more than anything.

This book would not exist without Morgan Woolverton, who turned me on to this music one fateful day in his black light–illuminated dorm room. He got me high as shit and played me this music as the cannabis overdose triggered a synesthetic episode that made me "see" the music. I hallucinated an epic battle between sword-wielding, rotoscoped monsters in helmets with nose guards, an experience that never lost its potency. It sucked me into the music for life, and it never would have happened without you.

Most of all, thank you to all the members of Anthrax, Megadeth, Metallica, and Slayer, past and present, for this music. It was hard at times to fully articulate what it's meant to me over the years, but I hope it comes through in these pages.

MB
SECTION
4
ROW
BIG
SEAT
ADMISSION
$
PRICE INCLUDES TAX
MB
SEC.
INDEX
4
BIG
SEAT

M

N

O

P

Quarto.com

First Published in 2026 by Motorbooks, an imprint of The Quarto Group,
100 Cummings Center, Suite 265-D, Beverly, MA 01915, USA.
T (978) 282-9590 F (978) 283-2742

EEA Representation, WTS Tax d.o.o.,
Žanova ulica 3, 4000 Kranj, Slovenia.
www.wts-tax.si

30 29 28 27 26 1 2 3 4 5

ISBN: 978-1-57715-819-6

Digital edition published in 2026
eISBN: 978-1-57715-821-9

Library of Congress Cataloging-in-Publication Data
Names: Bukszpan, Daniel author
Title: Heavy metal's big four : how Metallica, Anthrax, Slayer, and Megadeth transformed metal / Daniel Bukszpan.
Description: Beverly : Motorbooks, 2026. | Includes bibliographical references and index. | Summary: "Heavy Metal's Big Four shows how four bands created the wildly popular thrash movement in the early 1980s and remain relevant more than four decades later"— Provided by publisher.
Identifiers: LCCN 2026018640 | ISBN 9781577158196 hardcover | ISBN 9781577158219 ebook
Subjects: LCSH: Thrash metal (Music)—History and criticism | Heavy metal (Music)—History and criticism | Metallica (Musical group) | Anthrax (Musical group : U.S.) | Slayer (Musical group) | Megadeth (Musical group) | Rock music—1981-1990—History and criticism
Classification: LCC ML3534 .B84 2026 | DDC 781.66092/2—dc23/eng/20260421
LC record available at https://lccn.loc.gov/2026018640

Design: Cindy Samargia Laun

Printed in Guangdong, China TT082026